38/1000

Romans 8:28

Lyndell J. Emanuel - 2013

His Name Was Merle

Our Journey Through Alzheimer's Disease

Lynda J. Olander Converse

His Name Was Merle
©2013 Lynda J. Olander Converse

Library of Congress Control Number: 2013900502

ISBN: 9780615753720

Edited and designed by RootSky Books
www.rootskybooks.com

First Edition

Printed and bound in the United States of America

This book is dedicated to Mom who, in her caring, strength, and determination, has shown us what true love looks like

Contents

Acknowledgments

I want to thank and acknowledge so many people who played a role in making this book possible. To my siblings, no matter what any one of us in our rivalry may have done or not done, we all knew we were loved and we loved each other. Most of the time, we actually liked each other, as well. We learned from Mom and Dad what "family" is and how true love lives.

A special dedication goes to my son who has become the man he is because of who his grandfather, more than any other person or influence, was and how he lived.

I thank my husband for being the man he is — the man I truly believe God sent to take my hand and walk with me the rest of our life in a marriage that He has blessed. He is a man not unlike my own father; a man of principles, high morals, hardworking, honest, loving, and a bit stubborn.

I write this book in memory and honor of my sister who was the apple of her daddy's eye — the apple of all of our eyes. A unique person filled with love she shared with all, never judgmental and always supportive. You are truly missed, Sam, and will always be loved.

I thank all the children, grand and great-grandchildren, nieces, nephews, brothers and sisters, and aunts and uncles, of Dad who, with their combined support, made this journey less awful.

Friends Make A Difference

People need people,
And friends need friends,
And we all need love,
For a full life depends,
Not on vast riches,
Or great acclaim,
Not on success,
Or on worldly fame,
But just in knowing,
That someone cares,
And holds us close,
In their thoughts and prayers,
For the knowledge,
That we're understood,
Makes everyday living,
Feel wonderfully good.

— Unknown

Introduction

As I look back on my life and our family, I find it interesting and comforting that throughout our lives our best friends have typically been family members. Beyond that, we have all had friends who may not have been connected to us by blood or marriage, but they were like family all the same. A few of them are the kind of friends you hope you will have and know you can count on. But mostly it has been our family members down through the ages who have always been our best friends as well. Amazingly wonderful!

Without our family and friends this journey would have been much worse. We would have missed the many blessings throughout all the trials and tribulations. There were many times during this journey, I knew what might happen next and I knew we'd never be able to survive the next step. But somehow, we did. We continue to survive because of our great love for Dad and Mom and their love for us as well as our love for one another.

But I realize walking the Alzheimer's journey along with a beloved family member isn't just about the tremendous love and support family members can provide. Sometimes, we need a bit of information, just to help us along the way, give clues to what lies ahead, and lend comfort for all the emotions, challenges, and questions that arise.

That is why I've written this book. I searched for a book like this one, but could not find it. I have written the type of book I wish I had found when I was on this journey with my dad.

This is a loving tribute to our family, and especially my dad, but it is also a resource for you, as I hope you gain from our experience and find the hope, courage, and comfort in these pages to help you in some small way as you walk this path.

My hope is to help even one person get through his or her

journey and to keep the memory of my dad alive and well for everyone who knew and loved him.

Come visit with our family.

We walk with you.

CHAPTER 1

Snapshots of a Year

One of the pieces of information I wanted most to see when we went on our Alzheimer's journey was the story of the day-to-day interactions of others who had gone on a similar road. But I could not seem to find it. So I am sharing snippets of various days that happened over the course of a year. I share these moments as journal entries so you can look at your own experience and know that you are not alone. Seeing a loved one slowly forget you, become disconnected from reality, and grow increasingly confused happens to many of us. This is how it happened in our case.

January 2009

My brother, Larry, took Dad to the salvage yard in town yesterday to get the rear window for his truck. Dad and Mom had previously found one at the salvage yard that would fit his truck. He, evidently, had backed out of the garage to get a load of firewood. Without the garage door being open all the way, he broke the truck topper window.

The salvage yard had failed to get the window ready so they had a few hours to wait so they did some "guy" shopping and went out for lunch. Mom said they were gone about 3.5 hours. When they returned home, Larry stayed another two hours and installed the window. He said they had a good day — he heard many of the same stories several times but no problems or issues.

Dad, however, explained to Mom later about how BIG that town was. He said he'd not been there for many years and it's really gotten BIG. Mom is not sure where all they went but it sure was a BIG town, according to Dad. Mom enjoyed her day of catching up with her ironing. She even washed, dried, and ironed another load of laundry. She doesn't get many opportunities to just do what she needs to do as Dad gets confused if she's not focused on him all the time when he is around.

It was fairly common at this point in Dad's dementia for him not to realize he was at home. About 8:30 that night, he decided it was time to go home.

"OK, get your coat," Mom said. She got her coat and off they went down the road. Just past the lake Dad asked her where she wanted to go. She then asked him where he wanted to go. They agreed they should go home.

"Well, we better turn around then," Dad said.

They did and went home.

"Well, I think we should head on to bed," Mom said. "I'm tired."

They went to bed.

Mom has learned that when it's time to "go home" she has to make a U-turn in the driveway and go out the front drive because if she goes out the back drive Dad recognizes the house and decides he's home. Unfortunately, this realization doesn't last very long as he's not been gone long enough and pretty soon they have to go for another ride.

•

Each day is new and different and has its own set of challenges. I don't know how much longer Mom will be able to do this but she's determined to do it for as long as she possibly can and we have to let her. After all, it's their life and their quality of life. As much as I'd like her life to be a bit easier, easier is not always better. Her life is with Dad — in whatever way he is today. That is where Mom is happiest, or at least at peace with her decision. I have to respect her decisions and pray that I am able to help her when she's ready to discuss options.

My husband, Clint, made an appointment with the VA memory doctor today, which causes me some concern. He's not good about sharing his health concerns with me — mental, physical, or emotional. I asked if he was concerned or if he was just trying to establish a baseline for the future. He said he thought it would be a good idea to establish a baseline. He, like me, has a family history that includes Alzheimer's/dementia. Who knows what the future holds? Only GOD!

February 3, 2009

I had lunch with Mom, Dad, my son, Troy, and my daughter, Tamara, today. All are doing well, although Dad did not seem to be with us most of the time. He did not know Troy or Tamara. I'm not sure if he knew me, although he seemed to accept that it was OK for me to give him a hug and kiss and tell him, "I love you Dad."

I remember a few years ago when we were discussing the dementia of a couple of older family members and Dad asked, "Who are you without your memories?"

I have no answer for that question now any more than I did then. I just know, no matter what, I will always remember my Dad. That's probably much more important to me these days than to him but he does seem to know that he's at least supposed to know me and I'm grateful for that blessing.

Dad didn't eat very well today, which is the case when he is more confused than normal. He was very quiet and calm. I asked him if he was busy thinking.

He smiled and pointed to his head. "No, just absent."

"A little absent-minded today?" I asked.

He nodded. He still seems to understand that he does not know some things some times and that is hard to see but it is a blessing that he is still "with us" to that degree.

I talked with Mom this morning and she said they had to go for a ride again yesterday early evening. They picked up a pizza for supper and then he seemed to have his bearings a bit better.

Mom is amazing!

February 11, 2009

Mom called this morning, which is unusual as I usually call her at 8:30 every day. She wanted to let me know that she and Dad were going to go for a ride to town. Dad seems to be more confused today and he is not quite sure who she is but he's "fine." He is not typically irritable these days, just more "lost," often not knowing whether he's home or who Mom is. He is unable to recognize most of the family.

February 12, 2009

Sounds like Mom and Dad had a great day yesterday. A ride to Crosby for milk and cigarettes and since Dad was doing so well Mom suggested they go to the casino. Dad did well and they both had a great time. They had lunch and brought some of their money home. Dad is doing well this morning although he is a bit silly. He knows Mom and he "has a woman mending his holy socks" so he doesn't have to throw them away.

April 2, 2009

Dad is doing better this morning. The past week has not been as good. He frequently wants to "go home," "round up the pigs," or "go to work." Today, he wanted Mom to help him round up the pigs in the middle of the night but she convinced him they would do it in the morning. He agreed and went back to sleep but he did not forget.

In the morning he started talking about getting some crates for the pigs because he told the man he would get them rounded up. Mom finally said she would give him $100 for every damn pig he could find. He questioned that and then gave up rounding up pigs. The effort at redirecting Dad worked.

Dad used to like to watch westerns but now he doesn't and when they are on the television he doesn't want Mom going outside because "they are shooting" out there. She pointed out that there were no bodies but he still didn't want her to go out. Like she said, if it wasn't so sad it would be funny but she tries to see the humor in some of the things he does anyway.

Mom has arthritis that causes her quite a bit of pain. The cortisone shot seems to be helping with her wrist pain and that's very good. She needs some relief! She is committed to taking care of Dad for as long as she possibly can and I don't blame her one bit — he is her world and she is his!

July 2009

I have spent at least one or two nights a month with Mom and Dad for the last several months, which have given me some great moments with them as husband and wife. Moments I never would have experienced and memories I never would have had that I cherish; Dad calling Mom, "Babe" when he walks past and pats her back; the looks between them that let her know, he knows who she is today; and her smile that tells me she knows today will be a good day.

One of the funnier, albeit sad, moments was when we were watching a show on the television, about a winter survivalist in Sweden. Dad decided he had better build a fire before that snow and cold moved in. So, off he and I went with winter coats, splitting axe in hand to bring in some wood for the wood furnace. He seemed surprised to see green grass when we got outside, but he simply said, "Well it'll be snowing soon enough, we better get busy." I don't mind telling you I was sweating by the time we got the wood to the basement but

Dad built a great fire. Thankfully, he forgot to open the flue and the heat did not travel upstairs too much.

What was on the television was reality for Dad. People playing sports confused him as he thought they wanted him to play with them and he did not even know how to play. He often wondered why they kept showing up. Mom enjoyed television but she pretty much gave up watching it as it was so confusing for Dad.

July 12, 2009

I called Mom as usual and Dad was not having a good morning. In fact, it was a very bad morning. He woke up early and she didn't realize he was up. When she woke up, he was mad because she had been "gone." He wanted to know where she had been. She could not get him to understand that she had been there all the time and finally he got so angry he told her to pack her bags and get out. Then he took the car keys from her and told her she was not taking his car. Things simmered down a bit when she suggested they make his favorite apple/caramel rolls. Larry and his wife, Deb, stopped over for coffee and after a while, Dad told Mom, he guessed they should be getting home. She said, "OK but you will have to tell me the way," and off they went.

Larry and Deb went to their home and Mom and Dad headed out. When they got to the highway Mom asked which way now and Dad said, "Well, I guess we have to turn around and go back that way."

Mom said, "OK" and they headed back. When they got to the house, Mom got out of the car and went around to Dad's side before he got out.

"Where is that woman?" he asked.

"What woman?" Mom asked.

Dad said, "The one that drove us here."

"She left."

"How?"

"I don't know and I don't care," Mom said. "She's gone."

They went into the house where Dad continued to be confused but pleasant. He asked Mom what her name was and she asked him who he thought she was. He said he thought her name might be Audrey. That was good except he then asked her last name. She told him it was Olander and he laughed aloud and said, "That is really funny. We have the same last name!"

She said, "Yup, that's really funny."

At bedtime Mom wasn't sure what the situation would be since he did not seem to realize she was his wife and she thought she might have to sleep in the guest room, at least initially. At 9, she mentioned it was getting close to bedtime and Dad said, "Yup, 9:00 time for bed," and off he went.

Nothing more was said, so Mom climbed in the same bed and he kissed her. That was how she knew for sure he knew who she was, as he would not have kissed her if she had not been AUDREY — his wife!

July 13, 2009

Things are better today. Dad told Mom she was a sweetheart. That's a good indicator that he is not confused, at least not at the moment. I spent the night with them Tuesday and Wednesday and took them to the casino so Mom could catch a break. She relaxes when she can focus on the cha-ching of the slots. It's good for her, win or lose. It's a WIN!

While Dad and I were wandering around the casino, Dad had to use the rest room. It is amazing how quickly he can get out of sight. I was intently watching the restroom entrance for a long time and he never came out. Mom was playing "Lobstermania" when she realized we had both been gone from the area for too long so she headed toward the restroom entrance where I was waiting for Dad.

No Dad.

He was not at the entrance. Mom asked a man as he came out if anyone else was in the men's room. He said he didn't think so but he would go check. Mom described what Dad looked like to the man and he proceeded to look in the restroom for Dad. There was still no sign of him.

We started to panic. If he got confused, he would get angry. He would not know where he was or how he got there and who knows what would happen. Mom headed back toward her favorite machine in hopes Dad would remember it and go there while I walked and watched for him in the area by the rest room. All of a sudden, a neighbor woman who worked at the casino came dancing toward Mom with Dad in tow.

She said she'd found Dad wandering and he had told her he was looking for his dance partner. She told him she'd help him find her; they danced around toward Mom's favorite casino game, and sure enough, they found Dad's dance partner. He seemed so pleased and Mom was so very relieved and grateful.

The neighbor woman was aware Dad was having memory issues and knew exactly how to help him get back to Mom. What a blessing; another "hand of God" moment.

July 25, 2009

Dad has been having a bad time, very irritable and not recognizing most of us for any length of time. He is very angry and he thinks Mom is someone else and wants her to leave and get out of his house.

CHAPTER 2

Stories of My Father

When you see a loved one lose more and more of himself every day to Alzheimer's you want to find a way to somehow hold onto the person you know and love. If you are experiencing this now, one suggestion I have for you is that you collect a few stories of this person's life. You can collect them in a notebook or on a computer, in a smartphone, or using a recording device as you speak the stories into the device. It's not important what tool you use, only that you collect the stories.

These stories will lend comfort in the days ahead and may also even provide some means by which you can pay tribute to your special loved one, if you so desire. Don't let the sadness of each day steal those memories from you.

Here are some of my dad's stories.

1946 — Love

My dad, as I'm sure is true of your dad, was very special. Dad was the oldest son, second born of eight children. Mom was the baby of her family of five children. She had three brothers and one sister. The story of how my parents met is quite interesting.

They met at ages 16 and 18. Dad had been home on furlough before shipping out to the Philippine Islands as a medic in the US Army in 1945. Mom was taking the same train from Minnesota to California to see her boyfriend. It's my understanding that the boyfriend had agreed to provide Mom with the funds to get back to Minnesota if she'd come see him. "Back in the day" 16 was not too young to be considering marriage and apparently, the boyfriend had that thought in mind.

Dad noticed Mom, who was drop-dead gorgeous. Dad told us he watched over her like a guardian angel as he observed all the soldiers eyeing her. This is surprising because I have always seen my Dad as rather reserved and almost shy; protective nonetheless but not very forward when it came to women. At least that is how I have always thought of him. Regardless, he told us he was quite concerned about the other soldiers' intentions. However, as the conductor started loading the civilians and soldiers, Dad lost sight of Mom.

Once on board Dad flagged the conductor and informed him that he had loaded his "wife" on another car. The conductor apologized and led Dad to Mom, where she sat with the civilian passengers. Just as Dad had figured, a big old soldier was leaning over her making his pitch. Dad had often described the scene: "A big, burly guy was leaning over this pretty little woman, who resembled a scared a little rabbit."

Dad, not a particularly large man at 5'10" on his tallest day, quietly and politely walked up to the soldier and announced, as only my Dad could, that the woman the soldier was talking to was Dad's wife.

The soldier immediately apologized and moved away. Dad sat down next to Mom and by the time, the two arrived in California they knew they'd be together for the rest of their lives.

Dad took Mom to break up with her boyfriend. The boyfriend was none too happy and understandably, refused to give Mom the money for her return ticket to Minnesota. Dad helped her put enough money together to take the train back.

We are not sure how Dad raised the money, but we know it was honest because that's who Dad was, honest and hard-working. His love for his family came before everything else.

They were married July 26, 1947, and the rest, as they say, is history. Nevertheless, I will share some more of the stories and life's lessons along the way.

Mom Was Always First in Dad's Life

In my spiritual journeys I have read and learned we are to put God first, before everything and everyone else. I told that to Dad once and he said, "I would never put God or anyone before your mother." He was a believer too and he read the Good Book. However, he never read that he should put anyone before his wife. Mother was always first in Dad's life, as he was in hers.

When Mom was expecting me, her first pregnancy, she had what we women refer to as "a craving" for tomato soup. Dad always worked and worked hard but times were hard and money was very tight. They didn't have enough money for a can of tomato soup but there was no way he was not going to provide Mom with everything he possibly could so he went looking for a way to buy a can of tomato soup.

He picked up discarded soda pop bottles, which at the time had a deposit of one cent each when returned to the store. He found enough returnable bottles to buy a can of tomato soup for his wife.

This story is famous in our family and it's just one of many stories of how Dad and Mom taught us about family, love, life, and honesty.

I have many memories and stories to share, much like my dad. He shared stories of his childhood whenever we were together. It was just part of the dinner table conversation throughout my life.

One funny story was of his grandmother and him out picking berries. They were so engrossed in picking they didn't realize that a Native American was also picking berries in the same area. When Great-Grandma looked up and saw the Native American, she dropped her bucket and took off running leaving Dad, who was about two years old, behind. She ran back to get him to see the Native American running away in the opposite direction. He was just as afraid of the white man as the white man, or woman and baby in this case, was of him.

It's hard for me to imagine my dad having been alive that long ago but it really wasn't that long ago and the "Indians" as they were called then, were just like everyone else of that time, gathering the food God provided to take care of their families and trying to live a good life.

Dad, sharing this and other stories, gave us a sense of himself, his value system, and the importance of family. After all, Great-Grandma did come back for him.

Like so many of that time, my parents did not have much money but they always had their family, a roof overhead, and food to eat. They depended on and trusted each other. Sometimes they ate lard sandwiches, but they always had mealtime together as family. It was not so much about the food as it was about the family.

Hearing those stories made an impression on me and although life raising my two children was not the rose garden, white picket fence life I had hoped to provide for them, the experience of always having meals together as a family was important to me.

I passed this sense of family on to my children. They remember always knowing we would have breakfast together. Suppertime was always as soon after work as I could get it ready and we sat down to share the day and eat together. They know, as I always knew I could count on Mom and Dad, they could count on me. A very special gift from my childhood passed on to my children and now on to their children.

Take Your Daughter, Daddy

Daddy, Papa, Father, Dad, Pa. Whatever you may call him, Dad is special; especially it seems, to daughters. I am a daughter so that is my point of reference. Although I know my brothers each had their own unique relationship with Dad, my sister and I each had ours. She was a tomboy and liked to be outdoors with Dad. I was a girly girl and liked to primp, dress up, and try to look pretty.

Ever since I was old enough to talk, one of my expressions as we got ready to go anywhere was, "Take your daughter, Daddy."

I suspect I had heard Mom tell Dad to take his daughter when we got ready to go somewhere. I learned from her that Daddy was supposed to carry me, and carry me he did, throughout my entire life.

I was seven or eight years old when I developed a limp. My parents noticed it and took me to the doctor who sent me to Children's Hospital to see a specialist. He diagnosed Legg-Calvé-Perthes disease in both of my hips. At the time, it was

very rare, especially for girls. It was something I was born with and the best treatment at the time was undetermined. Therefore, until they figured out the best plan of care Dad carried me so I would not have to walk. I remember him carrying me whenever and wherever I had to go anywhere — yes even to the bathroom. I do not remember being told I would never get well, or that I had a disability or getting any special treatment.

People would come see us and bring coloring books and crayons, paper dolls and books for me because I spent a lot of time on the couch or in bed.

Finally, I got crutches! What a wonderful time. I could go anywhere, all by myself. Do not get me wrong. It was wonderful having Dad carrying me but it was so marvelous to be able to walk again!

People say kids are mean and bully other kids, especially kids with handicaps. I do not remember that ever being the case. I, the oldest of three at the time, took care to make sure my brother and sister did not get hurt. I remember some kids helped me. They carried my books and helped me get on and off the school bus. Other kids seemed to notice that and they helped, too.

I can only imagine what Mom and Dad went through during that time, not knowing what the future held for me. They never let it show that they did not know what to do or did not know how they were going to pay for whatever medical care I might need. What I remember is that nothing was any different. I was one of their kids and they loved and took care of all of us.

I learned years later Mom and Dad had been told that I might never again walk on my own; that I would never be able to run, jump, or dance. They were told I might need a full body cast for an uncertain length of time. How they took all that in and never let it affect us kids, I will never know. I never felt I could not do everything I wanted. Mom and Dad never told me there were things I would not be able to accomplish.

I never needed surgery, casts, or anything. Just the crutches for a year or so and then I was walking again. I walked, ran, and danced. I even jumped out of the hayloft once.

Life With My Dad

Dad was never so much about telling us how to live as he was about *showing* us by how he lived. Just do the right thing. He believed in Jesus and followed the Ten Commandments. The Golden Rule was his guideline: "Do unto others as you would have them do unto you." Dad lived by that rule and we learned from the example he and Mom set.

The first house Dad built for us. I remember family members helping him and knowing it was the biggest and nicest house ever.

Looking back, I remember one of the many jobs Dad had as he and Mom struggled to provide all that is required to raise a family of five children.

At the time, I guess I just thought it was what they did to

take good care of us. I didn't realize they struggled to make ends meet. Of course, being the kid I was, I always wanted more. I am sad about that today.

He'd found extra work during the late 50's cleaning businesses, scrubbing floors, dusting, washing windows, picking up trash, etc. The owner of the "five and dime," the Wal-Mart of that day, gave Dad the keys to the store. He trusted Dad to come and go as needed to do the work he was hired to do without supervision. Keep in mind there was no such thing as security cameras. He was trusted to open up and lock up. No one else was in the building except Dad. When I look back on it, I realize he was a bit at risk. If anything was ever missing or damaged he'd have been the likely suspect. Then again, knowing my Dad, he probably never gave that a thought. He just did the job diligently with the trust he had earned by the life he had lived.

Sometimes he would let my brother and me go with him and we would get to empty the trash into a bigger container for Dad to pick up when he was done with other things. When we were done with the work we'd all go to the store's lunch counter and Dad would buy us a snack — usually a mint patty and a glass of milk. He would always put money next to the cash register to pay for our snack. One time we asked him why he paid for it because no one would ever know we had a snack. He simply said, "I'd know." A teaching moment I never forgot.

Another time, I went to the corner store with my cousins. In those days a corner store was on almost every corner. They were mom-and-pop operations that catered to the neighborhood. Mom had given us each a nickel for a treat. We must have been very good kids that day. We bought our treat and walked back home. When we got home, my cousin showed me a bottle of fingernail polish she had gotten at the store. She did not have enough money for fingernail polish. She had stolen it! I was so upset I told my dad. He marched

her back to the store and made her tell the owner what she had done and return the polish.

Many years later, when my cousin was in her 50's she

told my dad how angry she had been at him at the time and for many years later. However, at some point she forgave him and was thankful for him and the lesson she learned because he made her return the polish. I was present when she told him how much she loved him; how much his life had influenced hers. I think that meant a lot to Dad.

Parenting is never easy, especially of someone else's children. Two of my cousins lived with us off and on over the years when we were all young. Mom and Dad treated them just like they did us, same rules and same love.

He taught us simple life lessons; tough love lessons that stand the test of time. I think we all have times when it's much easier to ignore things that make us uncomfortable and the decisions we really do not want to make. Rules we do not want to enforce when our children misbehave are always challenging. Doing the right thing is not easy most times. Nevertheless, when it is who you are and how you live it is just the way it is, you just do the right thing. That was my dad. He did not have to think about what was the right thing. He just knew because that is how his parents raised him and that is how he raised us.

Growing Up With Daddy's Hands

There was a country song years ago about daddy's hands." It is about the hands that had both tender love and strong discipline. I suppose in today's world the spankings we received, deservedly so, would be considered child abuse. Let me tell you though, I would much have preferred the spanking many times over the "talking to" dished out by Dad. He was a master at letting you know how your actions affected and disappointed all who loved you.

I lied to him one time. Well perhaps maybe more than one time but I truly only remember lying once. This particular time I was not home when I was supposed to be and I was with a boy. I was not on a date. We were not allowed to date until we were 16, but I was interested in the boy who drove the ice cream truck so I was a couple blocks from the house visiting with him while he was on his sales route. Mom and Dad had called all my friends to see where I was and no one knew. Unfortunately for me and fortunately for Mom and Dad, my uncle who had been visiting my parents had seen me and called them so they would not worry.

When I arrived home, Dad asked where I had been. I lied. I told him I was at my friend, Susan's house. Following the spanking and the verbal admonishment, I wrote Dad a note, apologizing for lying to him, for disappointing him and Mom and for causing them to worry about me. Mom, years later, told me Dad carried that note in his wallet for years.

I was truly sorry. I had disappointed the two people who always trusted and loved me. I remember thinking they would never trust me again. I was wrong about that; they did trust me again. That is the way with parents. They trust us. We hurt them and they still trust us if we give them a chance and show them we are trustworthy. We then have to earn the hundred percent trust that was freely given at our birth. That's a lesson I learned at daddy's hands.

Who Takes Their Kid Brother to a School Dance?

I cannot even imagine why in the world I thought it was cool to take my kid brother to my school dance. I must have been in seventh grade at the time. The Twist was all the rage and my brothers, sister, and I danced a lot at home. We had a record player and we all loved music and loved to dance. Mom and Dad always enjoyed watching us dance. We never thought about how well we danced. We just loved to dance.

I suppose it was because my redheaded little brother was so cute and such a good dancer I decided to take him with me to the school dance. No one objected so we went. No one else brought his or her little brother or sister that I remember, but my brother and I had a great time. We danced as people circled us and clapped to the music as we twisted the night away. It is a wonderful memory of my childhood and the support and love of Mom and Dad.

Sure, we had our sibling rivalries and troubles. But we also had the love and respect for each other that Mom and Dad had for each other and for each of us.

Sex and Sexuality

In the 60's there was something referred to as "free love." I, being a 60's kid, should have known about that. But fortunately, because of my parents, I missed the, "if it feels good, do it" philosophy. Thank God! I do not remember either Mom or Dad ever talking to me about sex or about what to do or not to do and the only birth control of the day was abstinence, as far as I know.

What I did know though was that if I behaved in a promiscuous way, Mom and Dad would know. Worse than them knowing, I would have let them down terribly. Somehow, they managed to relay to my sister and me premarital sex was not acceptable. We knew that having that experience for the first time was special and it should be with the person with whom we chose to spend the rest of our lives. I am not sure how either my sister or I survived the 60's without being part of all the "freedom" of that time, but we did and I have to credit our parents.

Others of the time may feel differently having had a completely different experience through the 60's but for me, Father knew best and to this day I am grateful for the love and strength he and Mom used raising all five of us.

Every Child Felt Favored

We kids have commented that we each know our parents differently. We each have parents that were at different stages of maturity and life lessons learned. Economics changed, access to opportunities changed, even the option to take a family vacation was something some of us never knew, but was the "norm" for my younger siblings.

Dad was stricter with the older three of us and a bit more understanding or lenient with the two younger boys; or maybe they were not as challenging. Understanding and disciplining each of us differently based on who we were must have been a challenge. My parents recognized those differences and raised us accordingly.

Each of my siblings and I think we were the "favorite child." I think that is an amazing testament to our parents. They loved each of us unconditionally and uniquely. We each felt that specialness without feeling that we had something our siblings did not. I do not remember ever thinking they loved one of us more than they loved the other. We knew that we each were special in our own way in Mom and Dad's eyes.

Dads Make Mistakes, Too

I hope I am not giving the impression that Dad and Mom were perfect parents and they never made mistakes. They are perfect in my eyes but they are also human. They did make mistakes. Marriage and having children are challenging and parents learn by doing just as much as they teach by doing.

Snowmobiling was all the rage in our part of the country

and every family's goal was to own a snowmobile. A company named Scorpion manufactured snowmobiles in our town and that made the desire even stronger to be part of the snowmobiling scene. It was family friendly in those days. The machines were not too fast, and made to haul the children along behind on sleds. There were no "groomed trails" in those days. We just headed off through parks and fields and across lakes with Mom, Dad, kids, neighbors, and food to cook when we got to a place that looked just right for a winter cook out.

We were on our way to just such a place when we discovered the lake we had to cross had started to thaw. Water was standing on top of the ice but the ice was still reasonably good, at least for snowmobiles and sleds. Therefore, we all headed out, increased our speed to cross a few extra wet areas and made it safely — albeit foolishly — to the other side of the lake. Unfortunately, a couple of snowmobiles got a bit wet and once we had stopped to marvel at our accomplishment for a few minutes the wet snowmobiles would not start. What to do?

Dad had a cigarette lighter so he took the spark plug out to dry it off, which would have worked except he dropped the spark plug. It fell into the engine compartment of the snowmobile. Dad tipped the sled up on its side so the spark plug would fall out from its hiding place, which it did. However, gas also ran out and when Dad lit his lighter a second time, Kaboom! The fumes caught on fire. We all frantically started throwing snow onto the snowmobile to put out the fire.

Once all settled down we mused at the error. We all knew that gas and fire did not mix, but in the moment, my dad did not think about that. Given the same situation again, any one of us might have done the same thing. Everyone makes mistakes, even dads.

Thankfully, no one was hurt, the snowmobile survived and finally started, and we had a joyous outing. We cooked our hot dogs over an intentionally started fire at the campground.

Lutefisk! Oyster Stew! Oofda! — Our Scandinavian Heritage Shone Brightly at Christmastime

Christmas was always very special at our house. We had wonderful Christmases with family Christmas Eve. We would all get dressed up in our best clothes and head to Grandma and Grandpa's (Dad's parents). It was so exciting. We would get to see all our cousins, aunts, and uncles. I remember the sounds and smells of Christmas.

Every year Dad's dad (Grandpa) would show Grandma, who was a wonderful cook, the best way to cook the Lutefisk. We could smell it cooking before we got in the house. I do not remember ever tasting it when I was growing up because it smelled so bad while cooking but all the old Swedes really liked it or at least acted as if they did. I think it was more about the butter and cream sauce than the fish. Grandma made oyster stew; again, I think it was more about the sauce than the oysters. I do enjoy a bit of Lutefisk these days though, perhaps because I am married to a Norwegian.

After a wonderful supper of many kinds of meats, mashed potatoes, vegetables, salads, cranberries, dressing, gravy, homemade bread, etc. we would all move into the living room. Dad's uncles would get out the fiddles and harmonicas. His aunt would sit down to the piano, and we would sing Christmas carols. Dad's aunt lost her eyesight shortly after birth but she learned to make music. She could play many instruments. One of her brothers had made an apparatus for her neck so she could play her harmonica while she had her accordion strapped on and played chords on that with her left hand and played melody on the piano with her right hand. Occasionally she would stop playing the harmonica and sing as well!

Many of Dad's family members were musical. Grandpa and his brothers all played the harmonica and a couple of the brothers played the fiddle. They all played instruments or sang or both. The same was true on Mom's side.

I remember Mom singing around the house a lot when we were growing up: "Oh You Beautiful Doll," "When I Go to Sleep I Never Count Sheep," and our favorite, "Chocolate Ice

Cream Cone," just to mention a few.

Sadly, Dad did not have those genes. He loved music though, almost as much as he loved life but he always said he could not even play the radio without getting static. You would probably have to be over 50 to see the humor of that statement. He did however learn to play the accordion after Mom bought him one for his birthday one year. She bought lessons for him too and he learned how to play a couple songs. We so enjoyed hearing him play.

After the singing Christmas Eve, the uncles passed out their gifts for each family, a bag of mixed nuts, assorted hard Christmas candy, a bag of oranges, and apples. We looked forward to the brown paper bags from the uncles every year. We always knew what was in them but it was still exciting. Memory-making moments, as my son would say today. They truly are wonderful memories. We learned and experienced how loved we were and the importance of family. We truly were rich.

We would open presents Christmas morning after waking Mom and Dad several times beginning around 3:00 a.m. What a wonderful time we had when they would finally get up. Mom would make coffee for them and we would all gather around our Christmas tree and open our gifts from Santa, Mom and Dad, and Mom's mother. Mom's dad had died when I was two years old so I do not have many memories of him. I do not remember him having given me a tricycle for my second birthday but I remember the tricycle. I had it for years.

The gifts were not elaborate but the time and the memories are precious. The toys are long gone or were broken. The clothes are worn-out or have been outgrown, but the memories... they last a lifetime and beyond.

Chreasters?

A slang term, probably with a negative connotation, used to describe people who only attend church at Christmas and Easter. We were "Chreasters."

We did not attend church at a building every Sunday. We attended church every day through our parents. We learned the difference between right and wrong, sin, and forgiveness. We learned about loving one another, Jesus, and God at home.

Christmas and Easter were simply times we dressed up and shared the same with all of our friends and relatives.

Perhaps everyone looks back on their childhood and reflects on "the good old days" with fondness and longing. I do not think of those days so much as the "good old days," but as days that made me who I am. Those days made me who I raised my children to be because of how Mom and Dad raised me. A heritage I hope passes on to my grandchildren and great-grandchildren.

We Looked Forward to Hand-Me-Downs

My mom's sister had all girls and they lived in the big city. They had lots of "neat" clothes. I always thought they had more money than we did. Actually, my aunt was a great garage sale shopper and seamstress. Because she was such a great shopper and her daughters were about the same ages and sizes as my sister and me, we got many great hand-me-down clothes. It was always so exciting when we would go visit them or they would visit us and we would get a big box of clothes! My sister did not care so much but I sure looked forward to "new clothes."

Mom was a wonderful seamstress, too. Whenever she had material she would sew my sister and me an outfit. She also made shirts for the boys. She made us matching fancy dresses for Christmas and Easter. She made dresses for our cousins just like our dresses.

The only other times we got new clothes were before school started in the fall of the year and at Christmas. We would all get a couple of outfits, new shoes, and underclothes. I know Mom and Dad saved their money and worked hard to buy the clothes and school supplies we needed. I never realized that "ricing" was what they did to make sure there was enough money for all we needed or wanted.

Mom and Dad Did Tough Work to Provide for Us

Ricing, the harvesting of wild rice, was very difficult. Two people would get in a canoe, one in the back to "pole" the canoe with one very long-handled pole that was pushed against the muddy bottom of the lake/bog to move the boat through the rice bed. The other person sat ahead of the person poling the canoe with a pair of "ricing sticks."

The "ricer" would bring the rice stalks over the canoe with one stick and gently tap the ripe rice off with the other stick knocking it into the canoe, alternating sides. The buyers would not buy green rice. The "poler" worked very hard to keep the canoe in the best rice. When the canoe was as full of rice as it could be without sinking, they would head to the landing to bag it so they could go get more or find a buyer. Buyers usually waited at the landing and bought the rice by the pound right away. Two hundred pounds a day was a very good day. I remember prices ranged from $.50 to $2 per pound depending on the quality and abundance of rice each year.

This might not sound too challenging but then there were the rice beards, which are like long, very fine needles, and rice worms that got under your clothing. Each ricer and poler had to tie their shirtsleeves and pant legs tight around their wrists and ankles to keep rice worms from getting inside their clothing. With kerchiefs around their necks and hats on their heads, they headed for the rice beds. Their efforts, however, did not keep the rice beards from working their way through the clothing and the worms from finding an entrance. Undoubtedly, when they arrived back home, they would have rice worms under their clothing and rice beards poking their skin through their clothing. Even more hazardous, was the possibility of tipping the canoe over and spilling all your rice, or falling through a bog when trying to find a safe and private place to get out of the canoe to go to the bathroom.

Silly me, I thought Mom and Dad went ricing because they enjoyed ricing. They mostly enjoyed being able to buy us new clothes for school so they tolerated ricing, rice beards, worms, and all.

We each got one more new outfit every year for Christmas.

We really looked forward to a nice warm winter outfit. That is probably why Dad cleaned the five and dime in addition to his regular jobs and whatever other work he could find.

He pumped gas, worked the iron ore mines, was a driver's license examiner for the state, logged and drove trucks. He worked pipeline, too, yet always had time for Mom, family, and friends.

It always amazed me how Mom could make such great meals out of very little. I remember knowing her grocery budget was very tight. Dad and Mom planted a big garden every year. Mom canned everything from beans to meat. It seems to me someone would come to our house every Sunday about dinnertime. No matter what Mom had prepared for us she managed to stretch it to make a fine feast that satisfied everyone. Perhaps that is why we had company every Sunday. I am sure it was more about spending time with Mom and Dad but the food was great.

Making Adult Decisions

I got a job in a nearby city and got an apartment with a couple of girls from school. After dating a few "big city" boys and finding out that not all boys were nice, I was pleased when my previous boyfriend showed up at my apartment. He asked me to marry him and I said, "YES!" I was not quite nineteen. He was a very nice young man and I think my parents were pleased at the time. It seemed to them I had made a good decision. I had been a good daughter. I had done things right and was on my way to being a mature and responsible wife and hopefully someday a mother.

They were proud grandparents when my daughter was born. Two years later, my son was born and by the time he was six years old my husband and I divorced. My parents were so disappointed and sad. They tried to understand how such a thing could happen. When you marry, you marry for life, as far as they were concerned. You figure things out, work things out. You do not just quit. That's how they had been raised and how they had tried to raise us. But it was the 70's and times were changing. Things were different; people were different. Mom and Dad just did not understand.

The truth is, we kids did not understand. The next 20 years must have been extremely difficult for my parents. They just kept on being my rock, never condoning what they may have thought was poor behavior but always loving their prodigal child. Because of their love and support, I finally figured out Mom and Dad did understand. The 70's were not as different as my generation thought. The 70's were just a handy excuse for those of us who enjoyed living on the edge and not accepting responsibility for our actions.

Mom and Dad endured challenges with each one of us kids, some to a greater degree than others. Nonetheless, they loved us. We always knew they loved us. Dad was famous for getting angry when one of us got hurt. I know it seems like a strange reaction to some but that was Dad. He would get angry because he just could not stand that one of his kids was hurt. When he realized we were OK, he would calm down and take care of the situation.

When I told him I was getting divorced again, he said to me, "If you change your name one more time, you're not getting mine back again!"

Now how is that for discipline? I knew he meant it and I had better get my life straightened out.

A few years later, one of my brothers talked with me about his need to tell Mom and Dad he was gay. He was worried about their reaction and he did not want them to be hurt or mad at him. I told him the first thing Dad would do was get mad. That is what Dad did when things were not as he wanted them to be; or he thought they should be. Then he would calm down and deal with situation.

I was wrong. The first thing Dad did was tell my brother how much he loved him. He was his son; he had always loved him and he always would love him. Dad never understood the gay lifestyle but he always loved his children. He always wanted the best for us and did his best to provide for us and to understand us.

Wisdom — Dad's Youth

Dad's wisdom always amazed me. He had only attended country school through the eighth grade. He did not like school much. He was very smart but a great student, he was not. He went to school every day because his parents insisted he attend. It surprised me to find out he did not get the best grades in school. He was very good with numbers and spelling and he knew history. He read a lot. I guess he was just always learning whether he was in a school building or not. Just like whether he was in a church or not, he knew the LORD. It is not the building you attend or the college degree; it is how you live your life and the lessons learned that are the measure of a person.

The Go-to Guy... Unless You Called Him From Jail

Dad was, from stories, I have heard and from my own experiences, everyone's go-to guy. It seemed everyone knew if Dad could help, he would and if you needed an ear or a shoulder he was the one to call. He had his values and principles, but he tried not to judge others, although there were those rare occasions.

Dad could not tolerate lies or liars. I remember him saying, "I can't believe anyone thinks I'm so stupid I'd believe their lies!" He was really quite offended when someone tried to lie to him. I always knew Dad had no time for liars, thieves, or cheats.

An example of Dad's go-to personality was evident even at a very young age. I found this excerpt in the booklet of memories written by my grandma, Dad's mother.

Life on Perry Lake

That summer was fine. He had work; we had cows, chickens, and lots of garden. Ole went hunting and we always had meat.

We had trouble getting a well there so had to haul our drinking water from the schoolhouse. Of course we always had the lake for washing and other things. Then in 1939, we had a bad winter; so much snow the roads were blocked at times.

I remember one day it snowed so bad that we were worried about the kids getting home from school, so Ole took a pail for water and walked to the schoolhouse to bring them home. When they left the schoolhouse the snow was way up to his hips and he had to break a trail for Merle and Phif and carry a five- gallon pail of water.

Merle said, "Here, Dad, let me make a trail." And he took the two lunch pails and plowed ahead on his hands and knees. But of course, he was so light that it didn't help at all. Of course, he thought he was helping Dad.

Excerpt from "Bits and Pieces of Our Lives Together with Our Family" by Elda Olander

•

So you see, even as a child, Dad was there to help the best he could. However, you did not want to call him from jail if you had broken the law.

One of Dad's younger brothers joined a group of guys who decided it would be fun to break into a store and steal some cigarettes and other miscellaneous items. When they

got caught, they were arrested and taken to jail. Whom do you call? You call your big brother, of course — or not.

Dad went to the jail and let his little brother know, in no uncertain terms, he was not bailing him out. Dad told him that he did not appreciate what he had done to dishonor their family name, of which he was very proud. Perhaps sitting in jail for a while would make my dad's brother think about what he had done and hopefully, when he got out he would be a better man.

Being the go-to guy is a lot different from being the pick-up-the-pieces-of-someone-else's-mess guy. Dad was understanding and tried not to be judgmental. That said, he also did not tolerate immoral or illegal behavior by his family. With love and his outstretched arms of forgiveness, he was always there once you realized the error of your ways.

Unconditional Love

My dad's brother wasn't the only one making mistakes. I was, also. I was a single parent and living a life foreign to the life I knew as a child and young adult. I finally realized I needed to change things and I became active in the Catholic faith.

I was not raised Catholic, however when I married my first husband I joined the Catholic Church. He and his family were Catholic and that was a common practice in the 1960's. As a married couple, we were not very active in the church but I went back to that church when my life and marriage fell apart. I became more aware of our Father in heaven and learned to refer to the priest as "Father."

During this time I was still struggling to find my way. I had found my way back to God in the Catholic Church and felt I needed to talk to the priest. For the life of me, I cannot remember exactly what the situation was, but I knew I needed to talk to Father. As I was praying and preparing to see the priest I realized what I really needed was to talk to my earthly father, my Dad. I phoned Mom and asked if Dad was around and he was. So I told her what was going on and that I needed to talk to him. She said, "Come on up, you know we are always here for you."

When I arrived, we had coffee and conversation and then Dad asked me to go for a walk with him. We walked and talked, talked and walked. I don't remember exactly what was said; I only remember he had time for me in the middle of a work day and helped me know that everything would be all right, that he and Mom loved me no matter what and they would always be there for me. He was exactly who I needed to talk to as always. I finally learned that life lesson and never forgot it.

What a gift! Throughout my spiritual journey I grew more deeply in love with my heavenly father, and I became reacquainted with the honest, moral, loving, disciplined lifestyle my earthly father had always lived.

The First Year of a Long Journey

There were tragedies along the way. The toughest was when lung cancer was diagnosed in my sister. That was November of 2000. She was 49. The doctors did not have much hope she would see her 50th birthday, which was in January.

Sandy, or Sam, as we liked to call her, was a deer hunter and the first female to hunt with the guys. Grandpa Ole referred to her as "that little feller." Opening day of deer season in 2000, she was at Mom and Dad's for the usual hunt when she received a phone call from her doctor. She had had some tests done. She had not told any of us about the lumps she had or the tests. That is just who she was, never wanted to cause anyone any worry or concern. Her doctor wanted to see her. Mom could tell by her actions that something was wrong, so Sam had to tell Mom what was going on. Sam met with her doctor the following Monday with the entourage of family members that was typical for us. We all got the bad news together.

What you have to know is, this was Sam. She was as close to a perfect child as possible. I do not say that because she is gone. She truly was the best child and sister. She caused Mom and Dad the least stress and worry and was the one we could all go to with our deepest, darkest secrets and troubles. She was my baby sister. It was devastating to all of us to have her be the one with cancer. We would all have traded places with her or donated an organ in a minute if that were possible. She was just very special to us all.

She was also a fighter. She was determined to live life to the fullest. She lived for eight more years fighting the cancer the doctor told her might take her in a matter of months.

Watching Out for the Other Guy

Truckers! Sometimes we hear horrible stories about truck drivers and the accidents involving them, I come from a family of truckers of whom I am very proud. Dad drove trucks. He drove, stringing trucks for pipeline construction through high ground, low ground, frozen, and thawed swamps. He drove semi-trucks hauling goods over four-lane highways, freeways, and through narrow city streets that required backing his 18-wheeler into alleyways that might have given a Volkswagen bug trouble. In addition, he drove a logging truck and pulled a "pup" trailer behind. He hauled timber after it was skidded out of the worst of the woods. He loaded it with the "clam" attached to his rig, secured his load and headed to his various destinations.

I never rode with him but I've heard stories about him and he was always being offered work so he must have been very good at his job. I heard it said once, "If you want a job done right, call Merle. He can turn that rig on a dime!"

Dad was a very good driver. After all, prior to becoming a

logger, he was a driver's license examiner. Another job he did with pride. He never had a car accident or a traffic ticket. He was awarded numerous safety awards as a stringing truck driver as well.

In all that, it is still amazing to me that he was able to keep his rig from, in all probability, absolutely flattening a woman who passed his rig in her little car at the most inopportune time.

Dad was hauling a big load of logs that required the use of the pup. The pup was a trailer about the same size as the trailer of the logging truck. It attached behind the truck trailer and was secured with a huge hitch and chains. We don't know how, but somehow the hitch came loose.

Dad could tell immediately that something was wrong as the entire rig started to sway. He figured out what had happened and knew he had to get the rig slowed down, stopped, and off the road. It was a two-lane road with quite a bit of traffic. All he could think about was what if the pup came loose while he was meeting someone or heaven forbid, what if someone tried to pass him as he was slowing down. Another nightmare scenario that went through his mind was with all the swaying, the load could easily have shifted enough to topple the truck and spill the logs all over the road and on any vehicles in the vicinity.

Of course the worst thing happened: A woman driving a small car decided Dad was traveling too slowly and decided to pass him. Mostly all he could do was continue slowing down and pray. He did both. The woman managed to get around him, probably never knowing how blessed she had just been, and Dad got the rig over to the shoulder as soon as he found a spot wide enough. He stopped without losing the pup or any logs.

He probably lost a few years of his life during those few moments but his main thought was not about his life. It was about what might happen to someone else. That was Dad. He was always putting the other person first.

The same caring Dad had for others was evident the day he and Mom came upon a car accident. They don't know what had happened but a car lay overturned in the ditch, still running. They could hear people screaming and crying.

In those days, there were no cell phones. Mom stayed up on the highway to flag someone down to go get help while Dad headed for the still running vehicle. I do not know all the details, and as you may or may not have experienced, at times such as these, people just do what they need to do. They do not remember all the things they did. Dad and Mom had that experience that day; they just did what had to be done. They just took the necessary action to help.

Somehow, Dad got the man and woman out of the car. He was taking a deep sigh of relief when he heard a baby crying! He had no idea where the baby was; when or if the car would catch on fire and explode; or when help would arrive. Had anyone even found help yet? He had to find that baby.

He started looking through broken windows as best he could, removing what he could in hopes he would not hurt the baby. He was finally able to remove enough of the windshield to see and reach inside the car and feel under the dash from where he thought the cries were coming. Bingo! He felt the baby. He called for Mom who came running as he stretched himself thin and long enough to get a hold of the baby and bring the baby up and out of the car — unhurt but very scared. Mom cradled the baby as Dad said prayers of thanks on his wobbly yet bended knees.

We never knew what happened to the parents of the baby. They were not local people so we never heard; they were airlifted to a bigger hospital. We do know, Dad with Mom's help, saved a baby that day. They have always been my heroes so it didn't surprise me the heroic action they took that day. I have my own visions of Mom frantically trying to stop traffic while Dad frantically tried to help accident victims, each knowing the other's heart as they tried to do what they knew needed to be done.

CHAPTER 3

The Realization That Alzheimer's Is Here

I've shared several stories from my dad's life, as well as my family's. These are all precious memories I've recorded here to remember the special times and even the challenging ones, as I treasure each. I hope these stories give you ideas for the types of memories you want to collect.

Now, I'll share stories about how Dad's condition progressed and we realized we had to seek treatment. Every family who finds out a loved one has Alzheimer's hopes and prays those moments of forgetfulness or confusion will go away or somehow be explained by something else less devastating.

We were no different.

I remember when Dad turned 75 Mom had a surprise birthday party for him. Chris, my youngest brother, had taken him fishing to celebrate his birthday while the rest of us got the house and food ready for the big surprise. All of Dad's brothers and sisters were invited and everyone came. They parked their cars behind the house near the big garage. What were we thinking? Dad would not notice all those cars when he returned with Chris and fish?

He noticed and immediately thought something had happened to Mom and he panicked. In the house he came looking like someone had just taken his best friend away when we all shouted surprise. He was a bit dumbfounded with all the action and terribly confused. As things settled down he relaxed a bit and made a valiant effort to enjoy his first ever birthday party. We could tell though that he was not OK, as he seemed a bit confused the rest of the day.

It was probably sometime later in the summer of 2006 when I noticed that Dad was developing more than normal age-appropriate forgetfulness.

As is typical, we all chose to ignore it and hope all was fine. Then one day Dad said to me, "I think I'm forgetting a lot. I can't seem to remember what I'm supposed to do sometimes."

We could no longer ignore what was happening.

I suggested that he and Mom go see a doctor since he'd had a brain tumor 20 years earlier. Perhaps there was something going on from that surgery. Maybe it was nothing except that he was getting a bit older but if it was something and he saw a doctor early enough perhaps it could be fixed. They agreed to make an appointment. I remember thinking it would be better to have the tumor come back than it would be to have some of the other options, like Alzheimer's disease or dementia. We have a family history of dementias so that was one of my first thoughts.

A few weeks later after a couple of visits and some cognitive ability testing it was determined that Dad was in the "moderate" stage of dementia, Alzheimer's specific. What a devastating blow. Dad did not seem to comprehend the diagnosis. All he could remember was that "expletive," doctor telling him he could not drive anymore. Dad got so very angry. "Who was he to tell me I can't drive? What does he know? I've been driving cars and trucks since I was 15 and testing people to get their driving license since before he was born!"

Dad continued to drive, as both he and Mom knew he was a good driver. He would forget where he was going sometimes but with Mom as his navigator they seemed to do OK. We were quite concerned and talked to them about it several times but it caused such anger in both of them we decided to back off for a while and pray that no one was hurt or injured.

In the meantime, someone — we do not know who — submitted a complaint or something to the state that Dad should not be driving. Perhaps it was the State Trooper who was called to a nearby town gas station/store to help Dad get home.

Evidently, Dad had taken the car without Mom knowing it — and ended up there, not knowing how he got there or where he was. He did however remember his wife's phone number and asked them to call her to come get him.

Shortly after that adventure, the DMV sent Dad a letter requesting he turn in his driver's license or come in and take a test to confirm his ability to drive safely. He was angry all over again.

Mom called and made an appointment for him after he settled down. They went to town and Dad took a written test. He failed. His dementia had gotten to the point he could not retain what he was reading so he could not comprehend the questions and consequently did not answer them correctly. He was very sad. He knew he was a good driver. He had never had an accident in his many years of driving. He decided to retake the written test in a week. By the time the week was up, he decided to turn in his license. It turns out they do not actually take your license as you can still use it for identification. He was very pleased and seemed to understand that although he still had a license in his wallet, he had to let Mom do all the driving.

This was another step in the journey we all thought we would never be able to handle. We did. Not well all the time but we got through it. Mom hated driving and Dad always told her what she was doing right or wrong, but they got through it.

Until that fateful day we had all been dreading.

The Day Dad Left Us

It was July 26, my parents' 62nd wedding anniversary. We all met at Mom and Dad's house with snacks and our gift to them: the Kitchen Aid mixer they had been shopping for along with a TV from Larry and Deb that fit the entertainment center. They were pleased and surprised, especially Mom, as Dad wasn't aware it was their anniversary. He did wonder, "Where did you find that mixer, we've looked all over." We could tell he was confused and I had a sense that we should not leave but we did, as did everyone else.

Fast forward to that evening, Dad became very angry. That strange woman — Mom — needed to get out of his house. He insisted she call 911 and get someone to come and remove her from the house or he would. She finally dialed the number and gave him the phone. The 911 operator was very good, recognized the situation, and asked to talk to "the woman" if she was still there. Dad gave Mom the phone and the operator said help was on the way.

The officer was amazing and connected well with Dad who then introduced, "my wife, Audrey," to the officer. Mom could have hit him with her shoe — after all he had just put her through, he now knew who she was. After a visit with the police office, Dad calmed down, although he did not know why she thought she could sleep in his bed later that night.

Dad slept with his clothes on all night.

They got through the next day and then it started all over again. The same scenario but this time Scott, the same officer, convinced Dad he should go see the doctor and find out what was going on since he had come out to their home two nights in a row. Dad said, "Well if I can see a doctor tonight, sure, let's go." He rode to the hospital with Chris and his wife, Karen.

Dad was a bit agitated later when he realized he had to spend the night but he finally slept. In the morning, he was extremely agitated and determined he was going home. He refused to talk to anyone, take meds, or allow vitals taken. I arrived about 7:30 a.m. after talking with the hospital to find my dad extremely angry. He refused to talk to me other than to say, "I'm going home!"

He did not know why he was there. When I tried to refresh his memory about the night before he absolutely didn't remember any of it. He said he would never try to throw Mother out of the house and asked what was wrong with my head? He asked if I wanted to dance with him. I said no.

"Do you want to sing?" He asked.

I said no.

I asked him if he wanted me to leave and he said, "Yes, you can leave."

I have described this day to my friends and family as, without a doubt, the worst day of my life. I have had some pretty horrific days in my life. I know there will be worse days ahead. From my perspective, I lost my dad this day. The man I had known as "Daddy" for 61 years left us on their 62nd wedding anniversary.

Our Family Faces a Different Reality

With the help of Dad's uncle, Beryl, and my brothers, Dad calmed enough to take his medication, including a sedative. He slept for a few hours, as doctors made the necessary arrangements to place him on a 72-hour hold and transport, by force if necessary, to a new short-term senior memory care facility in Staples called Lakewood Reflections. When Dad awoke he was very calm, receptive, and agreeable. He accepted that he had to go somewhere else to get some more tests done so we could help him. He actually got himself onto the gurney to get into the ambulance and off he went with hugs all around.

This was very tough but we were hopeful and on our way to getting help. None of us went to the facility in Staples. The doctors thought it would be best if we gave Dad and the caregivers an opportunity to connect without interference or distraction from us.

We agreed.

Making a Tough Transition

Dad awoke in Reflections and was extremely agitated. He threatened the staff, refused meds, meals, and vitals. I had spent the night with Mom, so I brought Dad's clothing and toiletries the next day, as requested by the staff. They shared with me how threatening Dad had been and that they were actually quite afraid of him.

I chose not to see him and we discussed some possible options. I suggested a male nurse try to work with Dad since he seemed to work better lately with males. I also mentioned, as suggested by Mom, they mention that Beryl, Dad's uncle and best friend, had called to remind him to take his medicine. The staff finally called Mom to get the OK to force a sedative that is quick melting if they could get it into his mouth. She OK'd the medication. We are not sure if they needed it or if the "Beryl" card worked but Dad calmed by lunchtime, took his meds, allowed vitals to be taken, and was reading the newspaper when I called later. Amazing!

During his time at Reflections, we watched Dad go through many stages. He was childish, agitated, loving, and understanding that people were trying to help his memory. At other times he was confused and wanting to go home. It was challenging.

One of my fondest memories of that time was the day he asked Mom to dance. I have a picture of them dancing to the radio in the activity room. It's a precious memory as they always loved dancing with each other.

The Journey Continues with Twists and Turns

We met with the doctor and staff to hear the progress and receive their recommendation as they listened to our concerns. We were all of the opinion that Dad needed to go into a long-term memory care facility. Of course, we hated to admit that, especially Mom who had always maintained that she would — and should — take care of Dad for as long as she absolutely could, no matter what it cost her emotionally, physically, or mentally.

She finally recognized that she had done all she could do and that Dad needed more help than any one person could provide — even his wife.

We leaned on each other for strength.

Role Reversal: Taking Care of the Man Who Had Always Taken Care of Us

We started making phone calls and filling out paperwork as needed to get Mom and me established as legal guardians for Dad, and to get the financial help needed to pay for the care he would need. Since I had been through this previously with my adult daughter, I knew of a few places and people to contact to get this ball rolling — and roll, it did.

We were on our way to getting the help we needed both for Mom and Dad which also helped all of us kids and all the grandkids and great-grandkids who were old enough to understand what was happening to Grandpa.

It was a gift to see the hand of God through all of this, as friends and family stepped up, lending support and understanding. At church Sunday, a dear friend shared her prayer for us: "Acceptance" was the word she shared. It was absolutely the word I needed to hear. I had prayed for patience, strength, wisdom, and guidance but I had never prayed for acceptance.

I certainly needed it.

We went to court to confirm Mom and me as Dad's guardians. This was very tough. Knowing it and putting it in writing were two different things. Telling a room full of strangers that your dad/husband is incapable of taking care of himself is hell! Nevertheless, we did what we had to do and God's hand was on us.

As we came out of the court and Mom was talking with the attorney I took a moment to play the message I had received during court from the social worker at Reflections. She was informing us that we needed to take a tour of Heartwood Senior Memory Care facility in Crosby. They had room for Dad and if it met our approval, we were supposed to pick out a room for Dad. I interrupted Mom and the attorney, another one of God's helpers, to share the good news. It had been too much to hope for that Dad would get to be in Crosby right away!

We arranged for the tour and picked out a room. The next step in the journey would be to let Dad know and get the details addressed as needed — bed, bedding, chair, towels, etc.

A New Kind of Family Event

Great-grandson Matthew's graduation/going away party a few days later was Mom's first family event without Dad. She did OK. She rode to the party with Chris and Karen, Zack and Reed.

Seeing Dad in a New Place

Visiting Dad at Reflections was very good. He was doing very well and shared some wonderful moments including that he knew these people were helping him with his memory. He made a few friends and became a "hugger" of all. He painted a wooden cutout sailboat of which he was very proud although he could not quite admit that he thought he did a good job.

Dad Settles in

Dad found his way into the staff update at Reflections, which turned out to be exactly what needed to happen — the hand of God! The doctor shared with Dad what was going to happen next and how it would all take place and that his family was going to be closer to him and able to visit him more often.

When I went to see Dad that afternoon he explained it all to me! I reminded him about bringing with him the sailboat he had painted and that we could hang it outside his apartment so everyone would know which apartment was his and he thought that was a very good idea. We had a very nice visit. Again, he shared with me how much the people at this place were helping him with his memory.

When I left, I told him I would see him the next day at his new apartment and we would have lunch with Mom who was there now getting things ready for him.

I reaffirmed that his apartment was in Crosby, which was his hometown. He seemed OK. Mom visited him a couple more times that week and was very pleased with his progress. One day when we were there together to visit Dad, after about an hour he said, "Well you probably have a lot of work to do and I know I do so maybe you should get going." He said it very nicely just being helpful, and we seized the moment and left.

Mom and I went to Heartwood to wait for Dad the next day. He arrived — with his sailboat tucked inside his shirt! We visited as we headed to his new apartment and put his things in the bedroom. We showed him around and explained that this was his new apartment and it was all his; he just giggled!

It was a moment I remember fondly.

We then went to the dining room for a wonderful lunch. Dad had a bacon cheeseburger, which he enjoyed very much, although he could not eat it all along with the French fries. We told him that was OK, as he was getting a bit chunky around the mid-section. We went back to the memory-care area to leave Dad with staff, to see the facility and to meet other staff. The facility was wonderfully warm and several of our relatives worked there, including one of Dad's nieces and one granddaughter. The hand of God was upon us!

Visiting Day with Dad

I spent the day with my daughter, Tamara and her son, Nigel. Nigel had to return to South Carolina on Saturday so we thought we would go visit Dad/Grandpa/Great-grandpa.

Mom called and my second oldest brother, Kevin, wanted to buy something for Dad's new apartment. Since Dad really liked music, we shopped for a radio/cassette player. We found one without too many bells and whistles. We all went to see Dad for a few minutes. Mom was there as were my brother Chris, his wife, Karen, and son, Zack. That was great because they could get the radio connected. The apartment was shaping up just fine and the sailboat was in the window box near the door along with the picture that Beryl took of Dad and the "big" fish he caught during their Canada fishing trip taken years earlier.

Where Did the Time Go?

I remember Mom and Dad's 25th wedding anniversary like it was yesterday. I was the oldest at age 24, quite young but then Mom and Dad married young at ages 17 and 19. We

all put money in the pot to purchase them a console stereo/ radio. It was a very nice piece of furniture and a luxury they would most likely not have purchased for themselves. They both loved music and loved to dance and we loved to watch them dance. We had a party for them in their backyard as July in Minnesota is a great time for outdoor events and the weather was perfect. Everyone we knew showed up to celebrate with them and we had a wonderful time sharing stories of their life from beginning to the day of the party and looking forward to the next 25 years with great anticipation of continued blessings and joy.

Their 50th wedding anniversary was a much bigger deal.

Who would have thought just 12 short years ago we'd be at this point?

I was now 49 and we all were a little more financially secure. We started putting money in the pot 12 months before the big day so we could host and cater a great event. We rented a facility, sent out open-house type invitations, and asked everyone to spread the word. Spread the word they did and we had hundreds of friends and family coming and going throughout the day.

We decorated the hall and created an archway to hold a reenactment of their marriage vows. As I mentioned earlier, we have a musical family. Two of my brothers sing beautifully as does my youngest brother's wife. They sang a couple of Mom and Dad's favorite songs. We all came together to "perform the wedding ceremony" and then we presented Mom and Dad with a memory quilt. We each had created a quilt block depicting one of our favorite memories from our childhood. We asked the adult grandchildren to do the same and those with children to incorporate their children into their memory block. Mom and Dad were very emotional; they held onto each other and shared their joy and pride and we all wept with the joy of the moment and the celebration of their 50 years of marriage that started with a train ride of two people from two different locations who became one in a way only hoped for by many.

I thought about all of those memories as I looked at our current reality. The quilt we made for that day held many priceless memories of a day gone by. My father may never again recall those many occasions, but we all would.

A Touching Moment

One of the residents at dad's new residence was a screamer. While Mom, Dad, and my sister-in-law, Deb, were trying to eat supper, the woman kept screaming to the point that no one could eat. Deb suggested they take their supper to Dad's apartment. As they walked past the woman, Dad, who had a little water left in his cup, threw it at the woman!

Mom could not believe it. As the woman reacted, Dad verbally fussed her out. Mom had a very difficult time redirecting him. The staff intervened, diffused the situation and helped Mom, Deb, and Dad to Dad's apartment. Of course, by then he was mad at Mom. She decided it best if she left. Deb stayed and helped Dad settle down.

Well, the next day, Mom and Dad were walking through the same area and there was the screamer again. Dad, being of a completely different frame of mind this day, walked up to her, looked her in the face, put his hand on her shoulder, and said his famous, "God bless you."

The woman immediately quit screaming. Her eyes moistened, and she calmed.

Mom asked her if she needed any help, if she wanted to sit down. She mumbled a bit of an answer as Mom and Dad walked her to a chair where she sat quietly as they told her they would see her later. That was another hand of God moment!

Making Adjustments at Home

Mom is sure she will never quit reaching over to see if Dad

is still in the bed in the middle of the night and mornings. I am sure she will never quit that either. After 62 years together in the same bed, it would be hard to break that habit and I don't think she should. Perhaps it's consoling for her to reach for him.

Mom is eating a little better. She actually said, "I hope your dad doesn't do so well that they think he can come home." I was glad to hear her realize she would not be able to take care of him. On the other hand, to this day, she wonders if she should have brought him home. She wonders if she could have helped him. I suspect she will always feel that way.

It's a journey she never ever dreamed she'd have to take and one she certainly wouldn't have chosen or wished for anyone, which is the same for all of us. Nonetheless, together we can do this for and with Dad. As much as Mom wants him home, she knows in her head that it's not an option. He changes minute by minute from being such a sweetheart/peach as Reflections called him, to being a bit "bucky," also as described by staff at Reflections. We have too much emotional connection to Dad to work through those "bucky" times without major heartache, which is just one of many reasons that he has to be in a long-term memory-care facility. Those "peach" moments, however, remind each of us of the man we know and love. Again, the hand of God. The journey is a bear but the hand of God makes it bearable sometimes.

Our Long Journey Continues

During the last year of my sister's life, Dad had progressed into the later stages of Alzheimer's disease. Her cancer was beginning to take over other parts of her body and she was less able to do the few things she'd been able to do for the past several years. She had a hard time breathing and she needed to have oxygen on hand. She was very weak and often times needed help to get from her room to the bathroom.

Fortunately, her son and his wife had purchased property that included a house where Sam and her daughter were able to live next door. Her daughter lived with her and was very helpful, a great comfort to Sam, and to Mom. Dad's progression was making it difficult for Mom to be with and help Sam as much as she would like to if Dad had been well. If Dad had been well, he and Mom would have been with her as much as possible to help her and take care of her.

Dad did not recognize most of us on any given day or hour much of the time that last year. He would, however, look at Sam, see her beautiful blue eyes and remember her as a baby. He would remember looking into those same blue eyes when she was very sick as a baby and he would be so sad. Then he would be happy remembering she had survived the illness. He would wonder where she was now, as he hadn't seen her for such a long time. Then he would want to go home. This was a very hard time for Mom.

At Sam's viewing the eve before her funeral, Mom was doing her very best to meet and greet and survive the moment as well as be watchful of Dad. Dad, on the other hand, did not really know where he was, who most of the people were and saddest of all, he did not know who "that fellow" was, referring to Sam in her casket.

He got quite angry when Mom was not ready to go home. He definitely was. His confusion combined with the fact that it was the coldest night in December that year caused Mom to be quite upset as well. He wanted to go. She wasn't ready to leave her daughter.

I can only imagine what it would be like to lose a child to cancer and because of another devastating illness, not have the support of your spouse of 62 years to help you deal with the grief. Mom dealt with it as she had dealt with the many traumas during the previous eight years of Sam's cancer and the long, arduous Alzheimer's journey with Dad. I pray that I have even half of her strength as life presents its unknown traumas in my journey.

As written by our brother, Kevin, after Sam's death December 18, 2008:

What can be said about our sister Sandy that really captures the amazing woman she has always been? I know she doesn't want us to go on and on here today, and to keep it short. I promise; I tried. Bear with me.

Sandy has always been a devoted daughter, a faithful sister, an unconditionally loving mother, a trusted and trustworthy friend. When I think about Sandy, and as I've tried to write down some of my thoughts about her, the words that come to mind most often are that she has always been resilient, and she has never been a quitter. Sandy has not always had an easy life. She has had to adapt and adjust in ways that many of us have never had to experience. She managed to raise two children on her own, and, like most of us who have been parents, that presented her with its own unique set of challenges. But Sandy always persevered and always supported and loved her kids. And they have rewarded her for all her efforts on their behalf.

Eight years ago, after all the struggles and eventual accomplishments and successes, Sandy was diagnosed with lung cancer. She didn't let that slow her down. She went back to school! Over the next few years she managed to complete her Associates Degree at Central Lakes College. She traveled. We were blessed to have Sandy and Lynda visit us not once, but two times, at our home in California. During those visits, Sandy enjoyed some "first-time" adventures and Michael and I will forever cherish those special memories. We drove down to Mexico where Sandy very quickly learned the fine art of haggling with street vendors and, even though she didn't speak a word of Spanish, nor did they speak a word of English, she negotiated some pretty incredible deals. It was an amazing thing to witness. She took in her first view of the Pacific Ocean and, after a little coaxing, even ventured in to the cold ocean water, and then very quickly said, "OK, I did it! Am I done now?" As many of us know, Sandy has never been one to get too experimental with the foods she liked and, at dinner one evening, we encouraged her to try an avocado from one of our trees, something she had never tasted before. After some reassuring that it wouldn't make her sick or anything, she took a few nibbles and finally admitted, "Yeah, that's pretty good." The next morning when I went downstairs to start the day and grab a cup of coffee with my sisters, there she was, sitting all by herself at the kitchen table, munching away on an avocado.

Sam has had a lot of support over the past few years in meeting the new challenges her cancer presented. My family especially recognizes Dr. Tim Yeh, who, through his extraordinary efforts, gave us the gift of eight amazing years with Sandy that none of us ever dreamed we would have. To the nurses, clinicians, staff, and many co-workers at Cuyuna Regional Medical Center, thank you all for your unending willingness to go so far above and beyond the call. Gale Templeton, I especially want to say God Bless You. Sandy was so blessed to be in your loving care.

I wasn't able to be with Sandy in her final days but we were able to talk by phone and my sister Lynda and my mom kept me in the loop as to how things were going for Sam. The one thing I was touched by, and forever will remember, was how her children, Damon and Jayme, were constantly there for their mother, attending to her in every way, watching over her, preparing her meal, doing whatever was needed, in the most loving, respectful way any parent could ever hope for. Damon and Jayme, you have honored your mother so fully for all she has done for you throughout your lives. For that, our entire family thanks you and we are all so proud of you. Teri, you have been there for Sandy and risen so consistently to the many issues and obstacles and challenges she has faced over these past years. What a testament to her life that the three of you were there for her, unconditionally and without hesitation. The easy path today, the path our sister would least want us to follow, is to be sad and to mourn. The better path, the road she herself would travel, is to be glad, to elevate our own and each others' spirits, to be so thankful for the time we've shared, the laughs we've enjoyed, the love which with we've been so very blessed. Sandy did not spend the last eight years of her life dying; she spent her last eight years living. In some ways, I think these were some of the best years of her life.

Sam, we will miss you so much, but we all take comfort in knowing that we will see you again, along with all the others in our families who have preceded you, and, when we do, once again we will laugh and play and tell stories and share all our beautiful, precious memories. Enjoy heaven, Sandy. You've earned it.

CHAPTER 4

Brief Moments of Smiles and Laughter Light the Way

When you are walking an Alzheimer's journey, you need some way to process your emotions, experience your grief, and collect your thoughts. As my family traveled our road, we found ways to deal with what we were experiencing.

One way that I will share and that I offer as advice to you, is to look for those moments to see your loved one's sense of humor or unique way of looking at the world. Recall those times. They can help you now.

Here, in this chapter, I share grief relief in the form of what we call Merleisms — quirky or funny things my dad said or did. Thinking back on those moments brings a smile to my lips.

•

Dad was so wise, understanding and strong — did I mention handsome? He was very handsome and he was very funny. He had a special kind of humor I reflect on with great love and admiration. In almost any situation, he could make you feel good or see the humor in life's travels.

I like to think I am an artist. I paint with oil on canvas and sometimes I create a nice work of art. Maybe I am an artist. Either way, we were at Mom and Dad's for supper one evening when Dad looked at me and said simply, "You're an artist?!"

I said, "I like to think so."

"Well," he said, "You work with colors. Do you like the color gray?"

I said, "Yes, you can do a lot with gray and you can make gray from any two complimentary colors like purple and yellow."

He said, "That's good because you're getting a lot of it!"

That was not where I was going with that conversation at all. I was getting gray though and he found a way to make it less traumatic for me. Unlike my sister, I've always been a bit vain. Dad would not let me spend too much time there as vanity was a pretty useless emotion. Self-respect was good; vanity, not so much.

I always thought Dad would live forever because he was so healthy and physically fit. He was limber and agile. He could actually clap the bottoms of his feet together, even when he was 80 years old. That pleased him as did his ability to put his foot up on the kitchen chair he was sitting on to clip his toenails.

The Alzheimer's type dementia diagnosis was devastating. I knew he would have a very long journey because he was so healthy. I was very sad. I did not want to lose him, and I could not imagine what his life and ours would be like. I know now that no one can ever imagine what his or her journey will be like. None of the things I thought would happen played out as I thought they would. Most didn't happen at all. We survived all of the things I thought we would never survive and the things I never even imagined; partly because of those special moments with Dad and his humor. Moments of tenderness, fleeting moments of the Dad we once had and being able to see him, touch him, and kiss his forehead.

Dad had a stroke a few months after going into the memory-care facility. It greatly affected his speech and his left side was immobile. He was left-handed so that really concerned all of us with regard to how much he would be able to regain use of it. He was unable to swallow.

During that time, we saw his humor occasionally. Because he was bedridden, nurses would come in every day and rub him with lotion after bathing him. The nurses loved him almost as much as we did and were very good to him. One day, as the nurse was rubbing lotion on him, evidently Dad thought she was rubbing a bit too much. Although Dad's speech was usually very difficult to understand, he said as clear as day, "You're going to rub all the hair off my legs."

Immediately the nurse said, "Merle, you don't have any hair on your legs."

He said, "Oh."

It was a moment of grief relief Mom cherishes to this day. She loves to share the story of his clear speech and his humor. Dad always had beautiful skin and he never had any hair on his legs.

After Dad's stroke, he had to go into a nursing home. The nursing home was very good about providing entertainment and activities for the residents. Dad was not able to participate in the activities but he sure could listen to the music. One particular family group would perform old-time country music. They all sang and played instruments from the parents down to the youngest child of two or three years old. They had violins, guitars, drums, accordions, and beautiful voices.

One day when this particular group was going to perform, Dad's sister and brother-in-law came to the nursing home to visit Dad and listen to the group along with Dad, Mom, and me. It was quite a wonderful day! One of those days, you remember with sad joy. We all enjoyed the music but we mostly enjoyed watching Dad enjoy the music. His enjoyment was obvious by his big, crooked smile. It was so great to know he knew what was going on around him. Mom told the leader of the group, who knew Dad, that Dad really liked fiddle music. Well that led to "Orange Blossom Special!" Dad started clapping, with his one hand, and tears started rolling out of his eyes. We had to laugh a bit at how funny he looked clapping with one hand as tears rolled down all of our faces. The joy and the sad combined to create an emotion I cannot describe and cannot write without experiencing it again even now.

We think Dad did not realize he was clapping one-handed. Although Dad was not an amputee, we think he had the phantom sense of his left hand clapping, which I understand is typical of people with amputations. While it looked funny, it was such an expression of his pleasure hearing the fiddle music that we were all filled with joy. That was grief relief. This moment and many others along the way helped to make the journey less painful. I pray you never have to take this journey, but if you do, I pray you hang onto these types of moments. They will go a long way to giving you strength and keeping you sane as you deal with the devastation of Alzheimer's disease.

•

A thought came to me one day when Dad was reaching and starring upward. I thought he might be reaching for Heaven; for those loved ones who had gone on ahead of him. Perhaps he could see them; perhaps they were calling him Home. Maybe he did not want to leave us but he knew he could not stay here. Maybe that is why he cried. Perhaps too, he knew he was on his way to that better place. We pondered that and it gave Mom and me both some peace.

We met with the hospital staff as it was determined since Dad was no longer benefitting from any type of rehabilitative services they would have to move him to the long-term care part of the nursing home. We hated to have him moved. We were fond of his nurses and aids. Nevertheless the reality was he was not going to get any better. During our conversation with the social worker, we talked about Dad and the future. The social worker shared with us that often times, when a person is coming into the final stages of their life, they have seen them reaching for the ceiling or sky and looking off into space Wow! Perhaps we were right. Perhaps Dad could see his family, Heaven, and angels.

The journey turned out not to be as long as I thought it would be given Dad's excellent health prior to Alzheimer's disease. I'm reminded of how often we think we know what the future might hold only to find out we don't have a clue. It really is not in our hands. We can only do our best and, I believe, trust in God. I felt the hand of God on us so many times throughout this journey. I look back and see His hand in so many events.

Perhaps we saw the hand of God even in the vomiting of all the nourishment Dad had been given over a period of days. A combination of humor mixed with the reality that the feeding tube was not working as well as we'd hoped. Mom was pushing Dad's wheelchair around the nursing home, as was her practice to do every day so Dad would see something other than the four walls of his room.

The charge nurse, who was a Green Bay Packer fan extraordinaire, came upon Mom and Dad on their usual outing and stopped to chat. He was wearing Green Bay Packer scrubs as he often did on game day. Mom was a devout Minnesota Vikings fan. The Vikings and Packers were lifelong adversaries. All of a sudden, Dad projectile vomited all over the head nurse and his Green Bay Packer scrubs!

We learned three things: The nurse had a great sense of humor, Dad most likely was not benefitting from the "food" he was getting through the feeding tube, and Dad either didn't think much of the Green Bay Packers or, as always, was standing up for Mom.

Now that was an event story that went around the nursing home and hospital quickly and for quite some time. It probably still is told occasionally on game day when the Green Bay Packers are playing.

CHAPTER 5

So Many Ups and Downs

The staff from Heartwood called Mom: They thought Dad had a stroke. He was transported by ambulance to the hospital.

I was on my way! I called the rest of the kids, the church for prayers and Troy, while driving to Crosby. Before I got to Crosby, Chris called my cell to tell me decisions needed to be made immediately about what to do as far as treatment options: They could give him a shot that could alleviate most of the potential stroke affects — but it could also kill him. They could airlift Dad to St. Cloud for monitoring.

On the other hand, we could just wait and see how badly the stroke had affected him.

We agreed to try the injection.

But by the time I got to the hospital, after spending some moments alone with my Dad, we were informed that Dad was not a candidate for the injection. We had no choice but to wait and see what happened and how well he recovered. They moved Dad to ICU with one to one staffing to monitor for choking and/or falling. Although he did not need ICU, monitoring there was their best option for care.

After Dad had a stroke, we had so many questions to consider. Many did not have easy answers.

Mom and I had opportunities to talk about the "what ifs" and share some stories. Mom and I didn't either one sleep much. We were up and ready to leave bright and early for the hospital. We arrived at the ICU about 8 a.m. Dad was well-monitored and the nurses were wonderful with him. They had learned, as had we that the best course of action in dealing with Dad was slow, soft-spoken, and gentle.

We saw a little movement of his left foot and toes. We knew he had feeling, as he got upset when Teri removed the tape from his left arm that was holding the IV in place. He said something like, "What the hell are you doing?" That was a good thing. He said some words and he could feel pain. Yes!

The speech therapist came and did a swallow test, which Dad failed.

Dad was sleeping most of the time. He had been moved from ICU out to the floor, but still had one-to-one staffing, as he was unable to swallow and he had to be monitored for choking. Mom sat with him most of the day from 8 a.m. until evening. There was no change.

The next day, Dad was still sleeping most of the time but he was awake for about an hour in the late afternoon and a bit "bucky." Earlier in the day, he awoke and looked at Mom. She thought he winked at her so she asked him if he was winking at her and he smiled and went back to sleep.

The speech therapist checked his swallowing ability again and Dad was still unable to swallow. The doctor checked in and informed Mom that Dad would not be able to go back to Heartwood. He was going to need care that facility did not provide. They were thinking Dad would need a feeding tube inserted. Mom was understandably concerned about what would happen next and what to expect. They said they would get a better handle on "what next" the following day when they did another swallow test and CT scan.

The next day, things were about the same. Dad was sleeping most of the time. We had asked for prayers for all of us, especially Mom. They were putting off considering inserting a feeding tube as Dad developed pneumonia. They put him on antibiotics.

Mom talked with some hospital staff as to what options to consider, including not inserting a feeding tube — if one was even an option anymore. They explained that with a feeding tube, at some point that would require another decision to remove it and sometimes that is more difficult than deciding not to insert one in the first place.

Mom and all of us wrestled with what that meant. I was leaning toward not inserting a feeding tube. Like one nurse said, "Merle is as good as he's going to be today." What if there was no quality of life to anticipate? Is there any value in a feeding tube? Tough reality!

Mom shared with me a moment she had when she asked Dad for a kiss. She said he cried. It broke her heart to see him cry as he tried to pucker up to give her a kiss. His kisses meant so much to her.

As we contemplated all the decisions that needed to be made, we got a lot of input from the medical professionals as well as well-meaning relatives. The bottom line was this was Mom's decision and she, more than anyone else, had to be at peace with whatever she decided. We siblings met at Mom and Dad's house that night with Kevin on the phone from California to share our thoughts and help her as best we could as she struggled with what was best for Dad.

We all had mixed emotions about letting him go but I think most of us believed it was the better thing to do. Dad would always be Dad, and he would always be "my dad" but Dad, as we knew him, was no longer with us.

Truth told, he had not been the "Dad" we knew for quite some time and now the physically healthy part of him was waning as well. He could not eat or move without help. His left side was paralyzed, and he was diapered and could not talk. However, those occasional smiles and open eyes kept us hanging on to what may or may not be reality. Perhaps his smiles were just automatic, like a baby reacts unwittingly to comfort, or gas.

I did not believe Dad would want to be like this and I didn't think he had the ability to let us know what he wanted. I knew he had always said, like many people, he didn't want to vegetate or go to a nursing home. He had been saying for quite some time that he wanted to go home.

I remember that morning, while lying in bed thinking about all of this, having the thought that the home he wanted to go to may not be his earthly home. Maybe it was time he went to see Sam, his mom and dad, brother and sister, aunts and uncles that had gone before him. Maybe it was time to let nature take its course and let him go.

Mom would miss him, holding his hand, kissing his face, and watching him sleep. She would never stop missing him. Sixty-two years of living with him would make that impossible, I believe. She would be given the strength she needed to carry on, as Dad would want her to do.

I said my "goodbye" to Dad the day he had his stroke. I told him we'd do all we could to take care of him and to help him the best we could, just the way he had always taken care of us. I told him we would take care of Mom until he could take care of her again. I told him I loved him.

Mom and I each held Dad as we prayed together for continued guidance and support as we proceeded through this journey. We thanked God for the many blessings and miracles we had experienced as we had seen His hand on us. We asked His forgiveness for the times we had not recognized His hand or seen His blessings. We prayed for acceptance of His will, whether Dad stayed here with us or went home to be with his mom/dad/brother/sister/and others and especially his daughter, Sam.

It was a wonderful moment and I'm so very blessed to have been able to share this time with Mom and Dad.

For so many questions, there sure are very few answers. Prayer! Dear God help us.

As a family, we decided to have a feeding tube inserted. That is a decision I hope never to experience again. It is very personal and very difficult. I believe it was the right one for our family and for Dad.

Dad's condition stabilized over the next few days, and he was able to have the feeding tube inserted. He would not be able to go back to memory care, though He needed to go to a nursing home where they could monitor him and provide his meds.

Moving to the Nursing Home

Dad would be able to get the medications IV, patch, or melt under the tongue tablets as well as IV liquids. His blood pressure was maintaining around 160, which was OK.

Over the next few weeks, we had several ups and down with Dad. One of the biggest pieces of news came as Thanksgiving approached.

Dad seemed to be doing better and Mom wanted to try feeding him by mouth again, no feeding tube. And it seemed to work!

I dashed off a note to the family, sharing the news. This is the email I sent:

FIRST — we're not supposed to get too excited so think with your medical side and pray with your heart side.

The speech pathologist, Jerry, was in to see Dad today as Mom had requested. He was going to see Dad at noon today but when he saw Mom this morning and asked if Dad was awake, and he was, Jerry said let's do this now because I really need him to be awake.

Again, don't get too excited... Jerry tried a little water in a straw and released it into Dad's mouth — he swallowed it! So then he tried a little applesauce or something. He swallowed a little of that and Jerry removed the balance of it out of his mouth.

He said to Mom, "Don't get too excited but he's way better than he was when I saw him in the hospital. I'm leaving instructions for the staff to have him up, awake and in his wheelchair tomorrow, Thursday, at 8 a.m. and Merle and I are going to the dining room for breakfast. Now, don't get your hopes up too high but we're going to try."

OK, my hopes aren't too high they are exactly the right "high," how about yours? Mom's are too so keep up the prayers.

Oh and guess where Mom will be tomorrow morning at 8

a.m.... you guessed it, having breakfast with Dad in the dining room. God is so good, and I give thanks for each and every moment as he keeps His hand on all of us!

•

Replies to my email from a couple of the granddaughters:

OK... I am in a controlled state of... freaking ecstatic!!!

You're right, God is so good to us. I will continue to pray that there is more good news tomorrow. Give Grandma a hug for me today and thanks for letting us know this. I know we may not get the news we want tomorrow and it's OK. I think what's going on, though, is a very positive sign and shows Grandpa's quality of life may improve and that makes me so happy. I'll try not to get over-excited, but this is really good news Lynda, so thank you so much.

Love,

Sarah

OK, so my hopes aren't too high!! But my spirits sure as hell are!!!! I've seen signs of this for the last couple weeks and I just knew there would be some good to come out of it eventually. That is so awesome!

The boys and I stopped in the other night and Dad was wide awake and so full of chatter. And 95 percent of everything he said was understandable. It was really good for the boys to see that.

Chris

That is GREAT news Lynda! Thank you for sharing.

I have seen Grandpa up in the chair a few times now with Grandma pushing him around. Most of the time he is sleepy, but we will keep up the prayers — they seem to be doing something!

Love ya,

Teri

The progress continued with Dad eating at least once most days. Mom was diligent about getting to the care center in time to feed him some Malt-O-Meal or Cream-of-Wheat. One day, they tried butterscotch pudding, which was one of Dad's favorites, at Jerry's suggestion. Dad was eating so well both Mom and Jerry lost track of how many bites he had eaten. As they discussed who was counting and how many bites, Dad clearly and plainly said, "Four... big ones!" Everyone heard him and everyone enjoyed the moment as they laughed with joy!

Dad continued to eat and respond appropriately, although he was sleeping much more than he was awake. Mom saw him every day and rolled him around the care center and hospital to see people and birds. When the LaSart Family singers performed in the activities room she made sure Dad was there to hear them sing and play. Dad always perked up when he heard them.

Thanksgiving dissolved into December and marched toward the anniversary of Sam's death, December 18. She did everything she could to make sure she did not spoil Christmas for us a year ago. Typical of Sam, she always watched out for everyone else; just like Dad in so many ways. She got her wish. We were able to make all the arrangements as she had wanted and have her funeral within a couple of days. It was however, the coldest day of the year. We then, as she insisted, celebrated Christmas with heavy hearts but we honored her wish. Thank you Sam for the Christmas we never would have had without your insistence and blessing.

Dad ended up in the hospital December 19, 2009, as he was vomiting a lot and the hospital had the medication and procedure needed to help him. They could not provide that kind of care in the care center. Mom, Chris, and Larry went in and stayed until about 11 p.m. Mom went back in the morning and stayed all day.

Dad went back to the care center after a few days. He had

some pneumonia, which was always present in one lung, now seemed to be in both lungs. The vomiting had slowed and he was put on antibiotics for the flu and the pneumonia. The care center/hospital had been overwhelmed with the stomach flu.

It was three days before Christmas and Mom, as usual, went to spend time with Dad. The care center recommended, for her own health, that she not stay. She peeked in on Dad and went home reluctantly. We were all very concerned about her as she did not sleep well and she insisted on being with Dad every possible moment. We were very proud of her and not surprised by her commitment to being with Dad and doing everything possible for him but we also prayed she stayed healthy throughout this part of the journey.

It was snowing the next day, with more expected. Mom was going to have Larry take her in to town to be with Dad at the care center. If she got sick, she got sick but she needed to be with him.

He was still vomiting; they turned off the feeding tube and put him on IV liquids instead while they kept him packed in ice to keep his temperature down. It had been running around 101.5 to 102 although once in the night they charted it as low-grade.

Christmas Day! They had never been apart for Christmas or for anything as far as that goes. Mom said Chris had dropped off bread flour and a beer last night so she could make her special bread. She decided to put the beer in her bedroom on the nightstand rather than have anyone open her fridge and think she had started drinking; very funny Mom!

Anyway, later she called Deb to have her come fix the bedroom TV, which she did but when she came out of the bedroom Mom noticed Deb looked somewhat confused. Then Mom realized that Deb must have noticed the beer on Mom's nightstand. Mom assured Deb, "No I've not taken to drinking" and explained why and how the beer was on the nightstand.

The funny little moments that relieve a bit of stress once in a while are sure helpful.

We all took turns spending time at the nursing home with Mom and Dad. We had decorated Dad's room the best we could to cheer everyone up. We hoped he would notice it was Christmas. He always enjoyed Christmas and Mom's decorations, especially her artful way of hanging tinsel on the tree he found for her every year.

The next 25 days were a series of highs and lows; smiles and tears as Dad struggled to stay alive and we all prayed for wisdom and strength.

CHAPTER 6

The End Comes

One Cold Winter's Day

Within a few days of the meeting to arrange to move Dad, his body started shutting down. The charge nurse, yes, the Green Bay Packer fan, called Mom in the very early morning of January 19, 2010 to tell her she needed to come to the nursing home. She called my brother and he called everyone else. We all arrived at the nursing home as quickly as possible, calling all of our respective children as well as Dad's siblings. We are a very big family. Because Dad was so loved, news of his waning travelled fast. The nursing home staff moved Dad to a very large private room so we could all be with him until the end.

Those that wanted were able to talk to, pray, kiss, and hold hands with Dad. We shared stories about him and our life with him throughout the day. Mom was finally able to tell Dad it was "OK" to go and that she would be all right. She told him, "Our kids will take good care of me." In the afternoon, the nurse checked Dad's vital signs. They were good. Someone convinced Mom to step outside and get some fresh air. While she was out Dad left us.

I believe, even in the condition he was in, he chose to leave while Mom was out of the room. He was always very protective of Mom and I think this was his final attempt to protect her. She was very angry with him for leaving when she was not by his side and to this day, she regrets leaving his room for even that few minutes.

We all tend to have regrets and guilt about things we did or did not do when we lose a loved one. My husband has always said guilt is a useless emotion. I believe he is right; it is absolutely debilitating in our struggle to deal with our losses. I suspect I will always believe this was Dad's way of protecting Mom right up until he died. Although Mom is very strong, Dad, in his quiet strength always looked out for her. I do not think he wanted her to have that final moment of his life on earth as her last memory of him. Mom's last moment with Dad, he was alive. She was holding his hand and kissing his forehead and looking into his eyes; perhaps getting one last glimpse of her lover, her spouse, her best friend for more than 62 years.

Following the flurry of activity that takes place at a nursing home when a resident dies, we all headed up to Mom and Dads' house to discuss again, "What's next?"

On the dirt road, which follows around the lake to their home, is a very old tree. Dad and his brother always called it the Eagle Tree when they were growing up; a dead tree that refuses to give up and stands tall on the edge of the lake in a swampy area. We have all seen an eagle in the very top of the tree on a limb that hangs out over the lake; a perfect perch for watching for lunch, no doubt. No one remembers ever seeing two eagles at the same time in the Eagle Tree. However, on this day, there were two eagles, one on the usual perch and a smaller eagle just one limb below.

What made this so unique or even mysterious is that Dad died on January 19th. My sister's birthday would have been on January 20th. She had died a year, a month and one day earlier. We commented that day that Dad had decided to be with Sam on her birthday. Seeing those two eagles gave some of us the thought that Dad and Sam were now together and they were just fine! We cherish this grief-relief moment, the hand of God, I believe.

A side note here — Sam's funeral was on the coldest day of the winter of 2008. Dad's funeral was on the worst ice day of the winter of 2010. I lived 60 miles from the church and it took me three hours to get to the funeral home. I had planned for it as I knew the roads were bad. My husband was sick so I had to drive by myself. I literally slid most of the way at between 5 mph and 35 mph. I remember praying, "Lord, You allowed this weather today, now you get me to the church on time!"

We all managed to get to both funerals in spite of the icy roads and the frigid weather.

We laugh now because Dad and Sam were both such easygoing, gentle-natured people they must have thought it appropriate to test us. They were probably watching over us to make sure we all made it safely to our respective destinations.

I'm reminded as I write this, Dad used to say, "Nothing good was ever easy." Perhaps as I reflect, it reaffirms what I've always known. Heaven is a better place. While this journey was never easy, both Dad and Sam are in a better place. We all continue to heal with our many wonderful memories of them both.

CHAPTER 7

Not All Questions Have Answers

One of the many things I learned during this time was that the patient and/or the family have to be diligent and that we truly were Dad's best advocates.

I felt his primary care physician had not shared enough information with us when we were in the decision-making mode about whether to have a feeding tube inserted, especially after speaking with the surgeon who performed the procedure. I was so angry: We had received so much different information, depending on who was talking. That was so confusing to us. We were trying to make the right decision and do the right thing for Dad, but how could we do that when those healthcare professionals seemed to be giving vastly different and conflicting information at every turn?

After visiting with the surgeon, I felt better, but still a bit angry because if I had had that conversation with the surgeon before, the decision would have been a no-brainer: It was an obvious choice that he needed to have a feeding tube. You can't just not feed somebody.

I had some new and very different thoughts about all of this. I had to reconsider my "advance directive" and talk some more with my husband. I do not want to be left to starve to death.

I'm beginning to think the "end of life" conversations may have an agenda that lead people/families to conclude that "letting" someone die is a noble gesture as opposed to doing all we can to give them the time they need to fight for life. Food and water are basic human rights and needs — people will eat bugs to have some nourishment, they will crawl on their hands and knees to get to water. As the surgeon pointed out, when it's your time to die, you'll die and there is nothing the doctors, feeding tubes or science can do to stop that from happening. I have always believed that and I do not know why I forgot that during all of this. That "damn" book the hospital provided to "help" us with this decision was full of misinformation, in my opinion.

It brought me back to the thought that perhaps there is a universal agenda to "let our elderly and sickly die" rather than help them fight. I've always believed our elderly were precious.

CHAPTER 8

A Legacy That Stretches Before Us

Being the oldest of five children, I had the good fortune of presenting Dad and Mom with their first grandchild. She was the most precious baby ever. I know, we all say that and we all believe it to be uniquely true; and it is, for all of us.

By the time my second child was on the way, my brother was expecting his first child and we were all off and running. Together the five of us gave our parents 15 grandchildren and, to-date, 21 great-grandchildren — all of whom know and love Grandpa Merle. They all have their own stories to share about Grandpa and how he influenced their lives. Their memories are precious.

Each one of them has a very special connection to Grandma and Grandpa unique to their experiences and personalities. For some it was hunting with Grandpa, for others it was Grandpa's wood working/carpentry skills. For others it was his spirituality, or his goodness, or his ability to teach and learn from life. For others, it was his love of music and his gift of storytelling of days gone by; stories we will all treasure forever.

A short while after Grandpa/Dad passed, Mom and I decided to see how much of his workroom we could sort through and clean. It was a very tough job as you can well imagine but a little at a time we were able to keep our emotions in check and try to get it done.

We found many treasures and "keen stuff," as Dad called them, that probably would not have meant much to others but most had a story or a memory for us. One treasure in particular was nestled inside an old tin cookie container. Mom did not know what it was until she took it out of the wrapping paper to discover the wedding cake topper from their wedding more than 64 years prior; overcome with emotion she did not know what to do next. She handed it to me and told me to get rid of it, as she could not look at it without missing Dad too much. It still had cake attached

to it, which was long since petrified and cemented to the topper. My removing the petrified cake scratched some of the black paint away. I cannot imagine how it survived all the moves over 64 years. Somehow, Dad had managed to keep it safe for us to discover at the perfect time.

With Mom's blessings I brought the topper home with me. I told her it needed to go to someone who would appreciate its value and sentiment. Whether or not it gets used again is irrelevant; it just needs to be passed on.

I remember one of Mom's concerns was that the grandchildren would not remember who Dad was before starting to lose his memory. I am certain they will never lose their memories of Grandpa. I believe when we have the opportunity to share our stories, our memories of Dad and Grandpa and Great-grandpa will be clear and wonderful.

Mom will be very pleased to know we have never forgotten who Dad was and how much he loved us, everyone! That is Dad's legacy, the love and respect of his wife, children, grandchildren and great-grandchildren; a life well lived.

Take My Daddy, Father

I can only share my memories of my childhood and my experiences with Dad. I am sure my brothers and my sister, God rest her soul, would have many more and different stories to share. I know, however, that we would all have stories of love and pride and thanksgiving for the parents God gave us. I am sure your Daddy loves you too, as much as mine loved me.

Unfortunately though, not everyone gets to know how loved they are by their father; some people are not able to express how much they love their children. Some fathers never even get to know their children and some children never get to know their father. My prayer is that you have

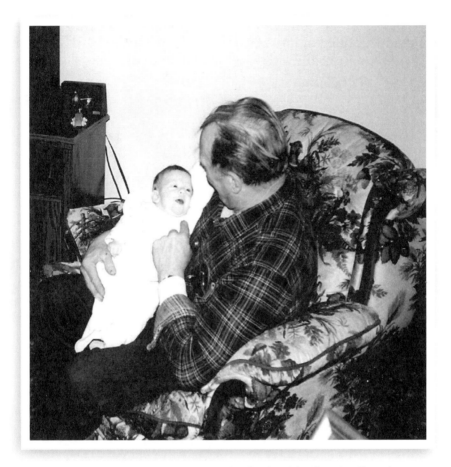

Dad loved babies. This picture is Dad with Sam's first born, a beautiful baby girl. I remember him always saying, "There is nothing more beautiful than a woman when she's pregnant."

the opportunity and blessing of knowing your earthly father's love. If that doesn't happen, I pray you have a father figure and that you know your Heavenly Father and the eternal, forgiving, unconditional love He has for you. It is my prayer that you will experience your earthly father's love some day because of the love of and for your Father in Heaven.

I have grown from "Take Your Daughter, Daddy" to "My

Father in Heaven, Take My Daddy." It has been a marvelously long and wonderful journey.

Thank you, Daddy!

Merle E. Olander
Born in Crosby, MN, January 5, 1928
Died in Crosby, MN, January 19, 2010

Almost a Whole Year Since Dad Died — Another Thought

I spent most of last night thinking; some good and some not so good thoughts. Mostly I am remembering times past. A big part of the thoughts are of the times after Dad's dementia started.

Last night I had thoughts about how much Mom did for so very long to keep Dad at home for as long as she could. We all were sure he needed more help than she could give him at home but she was determined to protect him and keep him from losing himself and his memory.

Mom would insist Dad could do the things he had always done, change oil in the vehicles, fix sink faucets and fences and doorknobs, install license plates on the vehicles, mow the lawn, etc. Dad would try and usually end up forgetting what he was supposed to be doing or what tool he came back in the house or garage to get. Mom would remind him and insist "he knew how" whatever it was he had set out to do, with her prompting.

One more grief-relief story here: Speaking of license plates, Dad had put the license plates on two of the vehicles about a year before he had to go into memory care. All was well and good, right? Well, after Dad died, Mom had to go to town for a few things. It was winter but a sunny day and the roads were good.

We did, however, have quite a bit of snow that year so when she attempted to get out of the parking lot she ended up in a field full of snow and off the end of the parking lot area. After several attempts, a man noticed her dilemma and offered his assistance. Someone else called law enforcement; they were not sure what the situation was exactly. In the process of checking out who Mom was and the vehicle she was driving, the officer asked her if she owned a pick-up. She said, yes but she never drove it, it was Dad's. Well the officer said it appeared that the license plates on the car she was driving belonged to the pick-up.

It turned out Dad had put the new license plates for the

car neatly tucked away on a shelf in the garage. Evidently, he had put the new plates for the pick-up on the car. We like to think, once in heaven, he realized his mistake and took action to get the help Mom needed to discover the error and rectify the situation. She did not get a ticket and we found the plates just as if the hand of God had directed us to them.

As I thought about all of this, I also knew how difficult it must have been for Mom. How frustrated they both must have gotten at times. Mom would get angry because Dad was not Dad and Dad would get angry because he could not remember and he did not know why or why Mom was angry. Mom would then be upset with herself for getting angry. She knew Dad could not help what was going on with him.

She was losing the man she married and loved for more than 63 years — and it made her sad and angry.

She hung on to every shred of time she had with Dad every minute of every day. She fought hard to keep what she knew and what she wanted. Her life, their life, was not what they had planned or expected in their golden years.

Once again, I am reminded of Dad asking, "Who are you without your memories?"

I cannot imagine what it would be like to realize you might be developing Alzheimer's disease; knowing there is nothing you can do to stop it. Also knowing that at some point, you will not know that you have the disease that makes you forget everyone you ever knew and loved. It is no wonder people with Alzheimer's disease get so very angry sometimes. I am sure there are moments when they realize something of what they have lost.

I tried to get Mom to go to support groups or read books about the disease to get some help and understanding about Alzheimer's disease and what was ahead but she would not participate. She said she'd read a little bit but what she learned in short order was that everyone's Alzheimer's disease was different and what anyone else had experienced was nothing she wanted to know about. I suspect knowing what she was experiencing was more than enough to have to know.

I have heard it said that you lose your loved one twice with Alzheimer's disease. You lose them to the disease and you lose them again when they die. I disagree. I think you lose your loved one a little bit at a time every minute of every day. I think it is extremely important to hang onto and reflect on the person you loved before the dementia in order to get through the long, hard days of the journey of Alzheimer's disease. If you believe, as I do, there is God and Heaven when your loved one dies, you know they are healed and have gone to the best place possible.

I believe I will see Dad again someday and he will be the perfect Dad I grew up knowing and loving and Mom will once again be with the man of her dreams. She will once again hear him call her "babe," and she will once again reply, "Oh Merle" as they lightly dance across Heaven in each other's arms.

God is good! Without my faith, this journey would have been unbearable, as would any future journeys that might present. I pray I never have to experience another similar journey but if that were the case, I know God will once again give us the strength, courage, and wisdom to survive.

What would I do if I learned I had this dreaded disease? Trust in God and survive according to His Will.

I pray our family's journey has done some small work to help you through whatever journey you are traveling.

Prayer for Those Who Have Gone Before

Eternal God, we praise you for the great company of all those who have finished their course in faith and now rest from their labor. We praise you for those dear to us whom we name in our hearts before you, especially we praise you for Dad, whom you have graciously received into your presence. To all of these, grant your peace. Let perpetual light shine upon them; and help us so to believe where we have not seen, that your presence may lead us through our years, and bring us at last with them into the joy of your home not made with hands but eternal in the heavens; through Jesus Christ our Lord. Amen.

About the Author

Lynda J. Olander Converse lives with her husband in rural central Minnesota. Combined, they have five children and 11 grandchildren.

The children living east, west and north afford them the opportunity to visit occasionally, but the Converses enjoy most of all when their children and grandchildren visit them in Minnesota.

Lynda, having retired from a variety of types of employment, now has the opportunity to share time with family members and on occasion be of assistance if needed. As an oil artist, Lynda has participated in several art shows and continues to paint when time allows.

If you have a desire to discuss your Alzheimer's journey with Lynda, you can contact her by email at Lyndac62@gmail.com. She would be happy to listen; and be a shoulder, if needed.

To learn more about the author, her work, and Alzheimer's Disease, visit www.lyndaconverse.com.